Contents

FOREWARD

"Jesus is coming...look busy!"

I have to admit the bumper sticker caught my attention, and even caused a momentary chuckle. But I quickly realized, with no small degree of sadness, that the Church really is "busy" these days—perhaps too busy.

Generations ago a humble Scottish preacher, Robert Murray M'Cheyne cautioned fellow saints, "No amount of activity in the King's service will ever make up for the neglect of the King Himself." M'Cheyne's words flooded my thoughts as I read Mark Geppert's provocative challenge, *Every Place Your Foot Shall Tread: The Attack Lambs.*

Years ago God used Mark to help my wife Dee and me prepare for a new role in heading the global ministry of Every Home for Christ, with a stated goal of taking the message of salvation in printed or recorded form to every home on earth.

Several years before assuming that role God made sure that Dee and I, and our two daughters Dena and Ginger, would cross paths with Mark Geppert in East Asia. God knew that meeting was vital to our preparation.

We were entering China (with contraband Bibles) when that first encounter occurred. Quite simply, our lives were forever changed. Traveling with Mark on a train across China is like experiencing a prayer meeting on rails. We prayed and shared, and then shared and prayed. But mostly we prayed.

Later, I was to link up with Mark in Warsaw, Poland, in the days immediately following the Chernobyl nuclear crisis (late April 1986) when the fallout was moving directly into the Polish capital. Mark had just arrived from the area where the explosion had actually occurred!

I was soon to discover that the very day the plant exploded, Mark was crying out to God in a large city square in Kiev, a proverbial stone's throw from Chernobyl. He had been asking Him to shake the Soviet Union with His glory and to open it freely to the Gospel.

Mark has been sitting and praying for hours under a huge statue of Nikolai Lenin (Soviet Communism's founder). It was almost noon, April 25, 1986. Suddenly, he was prompted by the Holy Spirit to stand and shake a clenched fist at the towering statue. "You're history, Lenin!" Mark cried. "You're history!"

Months after the disaster, which Soviet scholars would later conclude was a turning point for the emerging spirit of "glasnost" (openness) being orchestrated by then President Mikhail Gorbachev, I was able to do extensive research into the events surrounding that infamous late-April weekend in 1986.

Amazingly, it was within minutes of Mark Geppert's shaking his fist at the statue of Lenin that a single worker, testing the huge reactor which had been shut down some days earlier at the Chernobyl plant, made a seemingly minor mistake. That mistake set in motion events which by 1:23:58 a.m., just after midnight April 26, had become irreversible. In that instant the shaking began!

Interestingly, on the fifth anniversary of the disaster, the prestigious *Washington Post* newspaper would declare in its front page headline: "Chernobyl...is increasingly seen as the culminating moment in the collapse of a political and economic system that was both cruel and hopelessly inefficient" (Michael Dobbs, *Washington Post*, April 26, 1991, page one).

Indeed, by December 25, 1991 (Christmas Day, no less), President Gorbachev would officially sign a document formally dissolving the Soviet Union into 15 republics. Shortly thereafter, *Newsweek* magazine would report that so many statues of Lenin were being removed across the old USSR, there was a shortage of large cranes to do the job. In fact, it is said the huge statue in Kiev (no doubt the one where Mark had prayed) had a hand-painted sign written in Russian, attached to its base for several weeks which read, "We are sorry for any temporary inconvenience."

Today, because of the pioneering, prophetic prayers of apostolic warriors like Mark Geppert, Every Home for Christ has assisted the Church in the former Soviet Union in personally reaching over 26 million households with the Gospel. Throughout the region many hundreds of thousands of Russian lives have been transformed. Especially gratifying is the fact that 13 growing congregations have arisen just within a 60-mile radius of the doomed Chernobyl plant.

This is why I believe so strongly in the message Mark Geppert shares on the pages which follow. To me, Mark is an apostle of prophetic prayer who understands theologian Walter Wink's provocative and succinct statement, "History belongs to the intercessor!"

Every Place Your Foot Shall Tread: The Attack Lambs powerfully pictures the potential impact a gentle army of worshipping warriors can have on a lost and troubled world. I invite you, courageous reader, to join this gentle army of loving lambs and come help change the world.

Dr. Dick Eastman
International President
Every Home for Christ

PREFACE

Souls cry out to us. They are frightened children fleeing a gunman's mad assault or the faces of the aged trying to remember who they are. They are the anguished parents of addicted teens or they are middle-aged business executives who sense there is more to life than money.

If we are at all connected to those around us we ask many questions: How will they have a safer, better life? What makes people do the things they do? Where is this world headed? What is the Lord's will for my life and the lives of those around me? How can I get my kid off drugs? Is there going to be a place in heaven for my parents? These and many more questions are answered in the pages you are about to read. They contain some very simple truths that have become the Attack Lamb Lifestyle.

In the early seventies the Lord called me from a life in business to "preach My Gospel to the nations." I was very fortunate to have a pastor, Ray Patterson, who prayed every day and who confirmed that call from his prayer journal. I followed his example in the formative years of this ministry and found that if I addressed all things in prayer, the Lord would order my steps on successful mission journeys.

Obedience coupled with supportive church and family allowed me the liberty to follow the leading of the Holy Spirit in His purpose of taking Christ to the nations. From that ministry came the South East Asia Prayer Center which I currently serve. Our mission of creating new and networking existing prayer cells in South East Asia is fruit of many years of prayer walking, and the sacrifice of many people.

I have been very fortunate to see the hand of the Lord reaching to the lost of the world from the peaks of Nepal to the valleys of the Holy Land. On trains, planes, buses, ships and small boats He has been faithful to allow me to lead people to Him. In every place my foot has tread His power is manifest; but, my favorite thing to do is walk with a multi-lingual, multi-ethnic, multi-national team into a place where fewer than ten percent of the people know Who Jesus is and see the Lord break through in their lives.

I believe that the "bottom line" of spiritual warfare is "souls saved." We must get involved in the lives of those around us in as far as the Lord will allow us to travel. As you read this book, please do not think of me as anything more than a short, portly, middle-aged man who believes the Bible he reads and walks it out. If you can see yourself on a prayer journey, then by all means get involved. Please pray for your schools and your nation, and especially for the families in that nation.

If your feet wear out, as mine have, please email me. I know of a great set of insoles that can keep you going. Watch out for dogs. Keep your focus on Jesus. I'll see you one day in Tienenmen Square or at the U.N. or the White House. How 'bout a bowl of noodles in Hanoi or some of that wonderful sashlik in Kazakstan? Perhaps we will meet on the Nile or the Danube. Perhaps it will be on a street of gold.

When we do I'll be with a group. They will come from as many nations as possible and we will be speaking in many tongues. We will be glad to walk with you and stand before the throne. We will even let you stand in front because we love you and that is really why this book has been written.

Just one more word before you walk through these pages. If you are going to repeat any of the stories in this book, please keep them small. They have a tendency to grow with the telling and when they come back to me, I am embarrassed. Give the glory to Jesus. He is the only One worthy of the glory, and honor, and power, and might, and dominion. Please join me in walking before Him in every village and among every tribe. He'll be back soon.

Every Place Your Foot Shall Tread

The Attack Lambs

by Mark Geppert

With Bruce and Christine Wingard

CHAPTER 1

The Serpent is Bound

My traveling companion, an evangelical pastor, and I approached the guard station situated about a kilometer from the Chinese border. We were inside Laos on a weather beaten road, and had no papers to allow us entry into China. Wanting to pray as close to the China border as possible, perhaps being able to see into the land as we did, we felt this station might be as far as we dared go.

During the last several minutes Pastor had been telling me about how he didn't care for any of the "wierd stuff" we charismatics do, like praying in tongues. It made him very nervous. "Don't do any of that stuff, ok? No praying in tongues," he said. For the sake of harmony I agreed, feeling like a boxer who'd been told he can't throw his best punch. When we found a place to pray we stopped.

First, we worshiped but, in the back of my mind, I'm thinking, *"OK, Lord, how am I going to pray?"* As I worshiped I was released from the cares and doubts and worries of how I would pray, and surrendered myself to the sweetness of His presence. It was like my heavenly

Father and I were sitting together, indulging in our totally trusting and honest relationship. In those moments His Spirit touches ours in a way that wipes away fears and tears and gives us clarity.

A SIMPLE PRAYER

I opened my mouth to pray and out came a very simple prayer. "Lord, we pray that the Serpent would be bound in Laos." That was it. It was so simple, I repeated it again. For a moment I was tempted to be embarrassed, but I've learned that the most powerful prayer is the one the Holy Spirit prays through you. It was also accurate. Just how accurate I was to learn only a couple of hours later.

We didn't expect to be able to go into China so when the guard asked us if we wanted to go in we said, "No."

"You can go in if you like," he offered, not knowing about our lack of papers.

"We do not have the necessary papers," we explained, "but we would like to just go across the border and pray."

"You can go ahead," he replied, "I won't check your papers. Just make sure you come back."

As we walked the remaining "klick" to the border we were praising God. Once we were on China's soil we worshiped God and prayed for that nation. No praying in tongues here either, of course. After a short while we returned to the border station, much to the relief of the guard, though he gave no indication he was worried.

When we got back to the spot where we had prayed earlier we found a 12-foot python tied firmly to a tree. Wow! The Serpent really had been bound!

We asked around among the men at that place if they knew who had tied the snake to the tree. "We haven't seen anyone," they said. We asked them if they had ever known anyone to tie a snake to a tree like that. "No," they said. "When we catch a snake we kill him right there and cut him up for food." They had never seen such a thing, either.

Now I grant you it wasn't a burning bush; but, for us it might as well have been. God had demonstrated His commitment to answer our prayer.

Just recently I received a report that in the village just down the road from that spot, 200 people of the Aca tribe had received Christ from hearing only one cassette in their own language. Praise God!

We had attacked as lambs, quietly, without arrogance and in love, and God had given us the victory. If we had prayed in tongues or done some type of prophetic demonstration or made a declaration over the land, we would have missed God. Instead, we were acting in obedience to the Holy Spirit. We prayed the prayer He had instructed us to pray, as simple as it was. More importantly, our intercession sprang from the fountainhead of a worshipful attitude. Somewhere along the way the lesson that all successful spiritual endeavor comes as a result of an attitude of worship had seeped into our prayer bones and the 12-foot proof of its truth was right in front of us— tied to that tree.

GOING ON THE OFFENSIVE

This idea of a lamb being aggressive seems a bit strange, I know. After all, the very image of a lamb suggests it would be the least likely candidate for the role of attacker.

First of all, they are young. Then, they are small. They have no natural defense systems to speak of. They are not the brightest of critters, nor are they the fastest. All in all, they lack nearly everything necessary to take on successfully their natural enemies, the wolf or the bear. However, that is the point. Who would suspect such an unlikely animal to have the capability, let alone the desire, to go on the offensive against its enemies? Even if a lamb could somehow muster the desire, it still has no weapons with which to defend itself, let alone attack.

Oh, but if they could, wouldn't the wolf and the bear be in for a shock. Appearing harmless, but full of power and might. I know, not in this lifetime, right? No matter how hard we think about it nothing comes to mind as to how a lamb might transform itself into such an aggressive creature. And so, the question...

HOW?

How do you suppose a lamb might be victorious over, say a wolf? If you guessed run to the shepherd and let him fight your battle for you, you're right. It is the shepherd who has the rod and staff and slingshot, or maybe today a .357 magnum. The power resides with him. The lamb can make use of the shepherd's weapons, but not in its own strength. The lamb must rely on the strength of the shepherd.

So it is for us and our Good Shepherd Jesus. Yes, we have weapons of warfare to overcome our enemy, the Devil: the blood of Jesus, the word of our testimony, the name of Jesus, and the various gifts of the Holy Spirit. But these weapons all operate by the Holy Spirit who lives in us.

In us. There's a key! Unlike a lamb, we don't have to run far to find the Source of our power. He is **in us**. The Holy Spirit, God Himself, our Helper dwelling in us and working through us. Through us. There's another key! We don't secure the victory ourselves. It is the Holy Spirit within us who works **through us**.

What, then, is our part? That's simple...not necessarily easy, but it is simple. We have to train ourselves to be aligned with and sensitive to the prompting of the Holy Spirit. Then we must become obedient to His direction. It is simply a matter of teamwork.

ATTACKED BY A GATE?

Tradition says that as sheep we are to be meek and mild, give no offense, endure all things and return only love. Sounds pretty good, huh? But when these things are spoken of, it is in reference to our attitude toward others in the Body of Christ or the world which desperately needs Jesus.

Then what should our attitude be toward the realm of darkness, Satan's domain? In a word...ATTACK. Not in our own strength, but in the Lord's. Not at our own direction, but at His. And not with our own plan, with His. Remember He is the Lion of the Tribe of Judah, not us. But, some will protest, we are His Body. Doesn't that mean we do the fighting? Oh yes, indeed, but while the victory is ours, the battle is the Lord's. That means we fight the battle designed by the Lord, with His strategies, executing His plan, utilizing His resources and weapons. It's all up to our Commander-in-Chief Jesus, but we claim the victory!

Jesus gave us the definitive stance to take when He spoke to Simon Peter after his disciple's declaration of the revelation God gave him: **"You (Jesus) are the Christ, the Son of the Living God"** (Matthew 16:16 NKJV). After praising Simon and changing his name Jesus said, **"...upon this rock [of revelation], I will build my church, and the gates of hell shall not prevail against it"** (Matthew 16:18).

It is quite clear that Jesus' church and the gates of hell were going to come into a great conflict. I have just one question: when was the last time you were attacked by a gate?

Gates do not attack, they defend. They are solidly immobile. Their posts are dug down deep and set firmly. Gates are reinforced, locked and guarded to prevent successful entry. They are built to withstand attack; they do not initiate it. That's our job! We are to be taking the fight to the Enemy's territory in the power of the Holy Spirit.

We do that by becoming "Attack Lambs."

And how do we do **that**? Good question, thank you for asking because that is what this book is all about. It is painfully clear that the Body of Christ does not have within itself the power to defeat Satan. But the good news is we don't have to. Jesus has already done that for us.

What is happening in these last days is that we are learning how to enforce that defeat by stepping out of the way and letting God effect the victory through us, rather than trying to achieve it on our own. We are learning how to work **with** the Lord, to be attuned to His Holy Spirit and to walk in obedience to His direction. The result is...

WE WIN!

Say it to yourself. Say it out loud, "We win!" Let that fact that it's a done deal penetrate your thinking down to the floor of your soul. Let it take root there and continue on into the depths of your spirit man. We win.

The world system wants to convince us we can't win. We're only sheep. But, they're too late. We've already won. Jesus did that for us. It's like a friend of mine who had broken his ankle (twice actually), and the Lord healed it both times, in two different ways. It's too late to tell that man, "God doesn't heal anymore." He knows better; he has already experienced it.

So don't you believe it when the world tells you that you can't win. You already have! Jesus won the victory for you and, if you are a believer, it's yours!

Our job then is to walk in that victory. Again, simple, but not necessarily easy. Let's use the letters from the acrostic **W-I-N** to help us understand what the foundation of our success is.

WORSHIP

The first letter of **WIN** is **W**, which stands for worship. Worship is not only something we do; more importantly, it is an ongoing attitude we should have toward God. All successful spiritual endeavor comes forth from an attitude of worship. Why? Because as worship focuses us on the Lord, it brings clarity. This clarity causes us to see the affairs of this life for what they are. It releases us to see that we are seated in heavenly places in Christ, with Him at the right hand of the Father (Ephesians 2:6). We can see that the blood of Jesus has set us free from the presence and power of the Enemy (Hebrews 9:12).

Like so many endeavors in life, spiritual warfare has a mental side. In nearly every sport the mental game is far more important to ultimate victory than the skill level. So too, in spiritual warfare the mental attitude of worship is what sets us apart for victory and provides that non-skid foundation for our attack.

In worship, all fear is driven from us. We fellowship in our acceptance by the Father (Ephesians 1:6). We are righteous before the Almighty because of our Redeemer and the thought of it changes our being. In fact, as we join with Him through the worship experience, we begin to adopt His confidence, calling, and character.

His will becomes ours, His timing our timing, His power our power, His purity our purity, His vision our vision. Through worship we experience the effectual exchange of our nature for His nature. We are no longer lost in sin. We are no longer lost at all. We are no longer losers.

The fact that we can have intimate communion with the God of the universe through worship is a power connection we cannot do without. It is an uplink and a downlink at the same time. And it is vital to our success.

Unlike false gods, God wants us to know Him and His will. Every other religion on earth has a god that is hidden from the people. He dwells on a mountain top or in a shrouded holy place. He is inaccessible to mankind.

He is said to tower over the people and demand sacrifice that they may come up to him. Only Jesus has come down from heaven to meet us.

As we are incapable of attaining heaven through our own works, (which is the basis of all false religion), Jesus left heaven to reach us. This is the message of the Gospel. It is this fact which separates us as Christians from all other religions. This is good news for all mankind. There is a true God whose love has brought Him to earth to make the way of ascension for those who believe in Him.

THE SONG OF SURRENDER

As we mentioned earlier, one of our primary tasks is to align ourselves with the will of God. The will of God is not difficult to discern. In fact, here it is:

It is the will of God is that every man, woman, and child on the face of the earth have the opportunity to receive Jesus Christ as their personal Lord and Savior in this generation.

Obviously, the entire revealed will of the Father encompasses more than just this one statement, but nearly every aspect of His will and purpose marches under this banner. If the Father were to have a mission statement this would be it, the most quoted verse in the Bible, **"For God so loved the world, that he gave his only begotten Son, that whosoever believeth in him should not perish, but have everlasting life"** (John 3:16). This is the divine mandate for all of history.

But now we must come face to face with another question. How do **we** fit into this exalted purpose? It is so natural a question our minds assume it must be the right question. It's not. What we are really asking with this question is, how can I, with what talents and abilities I have, be used of God for His purposes? Wrong question.

THE RIGHT QUESTION

The right question is, (are you ready), am I available to God to be used by Him? Yes, of course, you answer. Not so fast, my good friend.

We are all kingdom builders, of one kind or another. Either His or ours. Most people try to build their own kingdom while paying homage to His. This will not work. Others try to develop a kingdom of their own within the kingdom of God. This will not work either.

The greatest prayer of Scripture, the Lord's Prayer, is the foundation of all spiritual warfare. Contained in it is one phrase which is the heart of worship, the song of surrender. It was the supreme prayer of Christ as He set His steps to the cross for you: **"Thy Kingdom come. Thy will be done in earth, as it is in heaven"** (Matthew 6:10).

For those who wish to chart their own course in the Kingdom, this is the end of the line. For those who would claim Christ's riches for their own extravagance, this is the bill of reckoning. And for those who try to heal the sick or raise the dead and count the percentages of success, this is the great humbler.

But, for those who will pray for others, live in humility and reach out to the lost, this is the anchor of their souls. You see, it is the surrendered life that the Lord can and will use. To whatever extent you lose your life for the sake of the gospel of Jesus, to that same extent you will find it anew in Him, in His glory, His power, and His passion. Your **availability** is far more important to the Father than your **ability**.

CALLED UP INTO HEAVEN

The reason John was called up into heaven to see the heavenly vision he describes in the book of Revelation was so he could see from the heavenly perspective. It was so he could see the heavenly purpose, and the heavenly worship which undergirds every declaration of the kingdom of God on the earth.

All the other religions of the earth have their hidden, inaccessible, mystical realms. Only Christ has opened the door to the heavenlies and calls us, not only to see but to enter in. Like John, we too have been called to see from a heavenly perspective.

Worship is key because it gives us the correct perspective. God's ways are higher than ours. His ways are perfect and our natural understanding is imperfect. But Paul tells us we have received **"the Spirit which is of God; that we might know the things that are freely given to us of God"** (1 Corinthians 2:12). In verse ten he declares that God has revealed these things to us by His Spirit.

God wants us to know His ways, His strategies, His methods, but He can only show them to us within the context of our relationship with Him, and worship is the material of that blood-bought relationship. Heaven is open to a worshiping heart.

As John was immediately **"in the Spirit,"** so we too, as we enter into worship according to His will, are caught up in the Holy Spirit. Sure, our body stays on the earth and we are certainly aware of our surroundings. In fact, we become more acutely aware as the power of the Holy Spirit to reveal the calamity of man begins to be activated. We are made aware, by the Holy Spirit, of the heavenly plan and purpose.

The things of earth grow strangely dim. In fact we no longer consider our previous preoccupations. Philippians 2 begins to live as we let the mind of Christ be in us. We think from a heavenly perspective and the heartbeat of God begins to set a pace for our lives. The rhythm of His heavenly Presence communicates that pace to our limbs, directing us in His plan.

IN THE SPIRIT

In the Spirit we are free from the desires of the flesh. "Me," "My," and "Mine" give way to "You, Lord." We worship "You" and the "I Am" begins to dwell in our praise. Just as in John's vision, all eyes turn to the One upon the throne.

Our purpose, our plan, and our presence fade away and His purpose, His plan, and His presence take their place.

Sweet surrender to the worship of God is the release necessary for you and me to truly become His ambassadors. Old things must pass away and all things must become new. We are the instruments of His will in the earth. That will becomes clear as we look upon His throne. No are no longer preoccupied with self; we can clearly hear what the Holy Spirit is saying, "Go ye into all the earth..."

When we are in the Spirit, we are limitless. There is no thought of purse or person. The cost of serving Him is nothing compared to His cost in serving us. He gave all for you and you know it in the Spirit. He is the only One worthy to receive blessing, honor, power and might. He is the only One who has defeated the Enemy and has taken His rightful place on the throne. When you are in the Spirit and you are worshiping Him, only His Person is accepted. You will bow down...gladly.

FOR THIS REASON

It is for this reason the trumpet call to worship has drawn you into His glorious presence so that you might be delivered from yourself, and be set free to participate in His majestic purpose. You bow down like everything else in John's vision. You are on your face before God.

In this position, you would never think of telling Him what to do. You only cry, "Holy, holy, holy" to the

One who is on that throne! There is no way you are going to think about a single care of this life when you are before the One. His grandeur answers all your questions for life. Will He provide? He is the Provider. Will He heal the sick? He is the Healer. No man will glory in His presence? No flesh will stand before Him. He is the only One talking in this picture.

Paul's letter to the Philippians declares,

That at the name of Jesus every knee should bow, of things in heaven, and things in earth, and things under the earth; and that every tongue should confess that Jesus Christ is Lord, to the glory of God the Father.

Philippians 2:10-11

When you are worshiping it doesn't matter where your problem comes from. It doesn't matter where it tries to hide. It doesn't even matter that the power which binds someone you care about might be from the Devil himself? When you are in the Spirit, you know that power is going to bow down at the mention of that glorious name, JESUS!

When our focus is on the One who is on the throne our message is based upon His victory. Lenin is in his tomb. Mao is in his tomb. I have visited the bones of Buddha in his tomb. Mohammed is in his tomb. But Jesus rose from His tomb to prove He was the Son of God. His victory over death validates His claim of Messiahship. As the Scripture says, **it is by grace we are saved, through faith, *and that not of ourselves*, but it is a gift of God** (Ephesians 2:9 emphasis added). When a man tells me that he can get to heaven by his works, I realize either he has a very dim view of heaven or a overly bright view of himself.

THE DEVIL'S LIE

The movie *Star Wars* popularized the concept that the spiritual realm has two equal sides to it, one good and one evil. A light side and a dark side, if you will. The assumption made was that they were both more or less equal, with right on the side of light, and cunning on the dark side. Luke Skywalker was constantly being tempted to join the dark side because its power seemed stronger. In the end, however, Hollywood gave the victory to the good side of the force, (it's a better story that way), and we were left with the feeling that the light side had somehow pulled out a win over a much superior force.

In the real world of the spirit nothing could be farther from the truth. While the Devil would love to have you believe he is the negative, and therefore equal opposite, of Jesus Christ, it just isn't true.

Jesus has always existed with the Father.

Satan is merely a created being.

Jesus has authentic spiritual power.

Satan can only counterfeit, lie and deceive.

Jesus has a home in heaven.

Satan was cast down from heaven.

All power and authority was given to Jesus in heaven and earth.

Satan has no authority except what we give him.

Jesus is the equal of God and is God.

Satan is merely a defeated and fallen angel.

And we are the ones who will judge the angels.

THE ABSURD ASSERTION

To assert, therefore, that Jesus and Satan are opposite equals is totally absurd. In fact, the Devil isn't even present in the vision John has of heaven. But guess what? We are. That's right. People were there doing what Satan would not: worshiping the Lord. When we worship the Lord we are giving to Him the very thing Satan covets for himself. No wonder worship upsets him so. The truth is, as a pastor friend of mine puts it, "Greaaaat BIG God. Little bitty devil."

You belong in heaven. The Devil doesn't. You were made to operate effectively in the kingdom of heaven here on earth. He can't. You can operate in Jesus' full authority, using the Name of the King of the universe to overcome the tide of evil in this world. And, your Enemy has already been defeated by the very One in whose name you operate, Jesus.

We are a part of a heavenly celebration. Jesus has given us great victory. We are in the earth to celebrate that victory before God and a defeated Enemy. When we go out to pray as Attack Lambs, we are not going to gain a victory. We are going to celebrate a victory that has already been won. Hallelujah!

CHAPTER 2
The 90% Solution

W e stood behind a wide yellow line. It was painted on the floor and up the walls of the two-story cell block in the Armstrong County jail in Kittanning, Pennsylvania. Rows of cells lined the walls of the big room on either side of us and stacked above them was another row of cells. I didn't know what the temperature was, but it felt cold; cold in my soul. Concrete and steel were the only sights to see. The guards straddled the line as the cell doors clanged open and they called to the men to come out. But the inmates just called back insults from behind the barred cells.

"What do we do now," I wondered? We had come with hearts filled with hope and compassion for these men, but their hardness was a slap in our faces. No one moved from their cells. The ministry team was looking to me, their pastor, for leadership. "Tell us what to do," their eyes said. I didn't know.

In my heart I could feel the love of Jesus for these men, and His compassion to see them freed. I could see Him, the King of kings, proclaiming their release and out of my spirit, at the prompting of the Holy Spirit within, I began to sing. The team joined in and we sang the anthem of heaven in praise to Jesus. "Holy, holy, holy Lord, God of power and might, heaven and earth are filled with your glory..."

After a few moments the jeers and insults stopped. A soft shuffling sound began as men slowly emerged from their cells. Warm tears started flowing from closed eyelids and cascading down uplifted faces as the loving presence of God entered this man-made hell. His glory filled the place and saturated the very walls. The shuffling sound of feet on concrete became entwined with the sound of angel's wings as we sang. I had obeyed the simplest of promptings and God had poured Himself out to them.

Opening my eyes, I was aware of the faces of those who had been touched by God, but my attention was drawn above them to an area at the top of the flight of metal steps which connected the upper and lower cell blocks. There I saw a white Figure, brilliant in sparkling silver and pure white light. He was taller than eight feet and His face was light energy without describable feature. As we sang, there emanated from the folds of His flowing robe a cloud-like presence which flowed down the stairs and throughout the main floor of the cell block and into each and every cell. Every man there was touched.

The effect of this Presence was deliverance. Hardened men wept as we continued to sing praises to the Lord. They confessed sin. They found forgiveness. They opened their hearts to the Lord. They declared His glory. They entered into the presence and will of God. This heavenly vision was a reality on earth as that night Jesus visited that jail.

Someone smarter than I has said, "90 percent of almost anything is just showing up." It was surely true that night. We did nothing more than show up and do our 10 percent. And that consisted of singing the song He prompted us to sing. God did the rest. So it is with our next foundation block for success.

GAP STANDERS

As we drove home, I realized in an even greater way the call of God on my life. I realized that He needs people to go into the prisons of the earth and proclaim His glory among the heathen. I realized that Jesus was moving in a mighty way and that the most hardened of men would melt in His presence. He just needed someone to go and sing that song, pray that prayer, reach out to that man, take that territory for Him.

I became aware in that instant that the One at the head of the stairs was able to reach to the farthest corner of that cell block, or to the ends of the earth to save, or heal and deliver as long as one of His witnesses would go out and sing His praises before the heathen. That night it was actual singing, but showing forth His glory could have taken many forms.

After an experience like that it would have been tempting to start a "singing ministry," but I did not form a band, hire backup singers or get an agent. I took that heavenly song and vision and through His direction and provision began to travel around the world praising Him. We've done it both in sanctuaries and streets. I have seen Him do the impossible for rich and poor, simple and wise. Jesus continues to use those who will go forth, and He backs up His Word with signs and wonders.

What happened that day in the Armstrong County jail is really simple. A large gap existed between those men and God. God needed someone to come and fill that gap, to pray on behalf of those men for their reconciliation to God. We were available, and with no special talent or abilities, (if you've ever heard my singing you would know how true this is), we were able to stand in the gap for those men. Then God Himself bridged the gap of sin and brought salvation and true freedom to the captives.

A "gap" is a space between two places. For most people that gap is between where they are spiritually and where they ought to be. I'm glad that you are thinking about others. That is really good. As long as you are aware there are gaps in your life, you will have the humility to pray for the gaps in others. The hard question is, are you willing to stand in those gaps for them? Those gaps create the doorways through which the enemy's lies enter in.

HOW GAPS DEVELOP

The soul of man longs for the fulfilling presence of God. Man, however, entertains other desires that lead to fulfillment apart from Christ and, therefore, to sin. Sin is fundamentally the fulfillment of lust. When any other person, place, or thing is substituted for the fulfilling presence of God, disappointment will follow as surely as wet follows rain.

A person without Christ is not able to access the heavens and receive from God. It's like trying to tune in a TV when you don't have an antenna; there is no established uplink. God only responds to one prayer of the sinner: one special prayer that confesses and repents of a sinful state and asks forgiveness; the prayer that asks Jesus to be Lord and Savior. With that prayer, all of heaven's benefits become available and the gap is closed.

When people look for the perfect church, they begin by attending services. Eventually they affirm that God is indeed in their midst. They decide to stay a while and begin to build relationship. They begin to put their trust in the pastor or another leader of the fellowship. Along with the joy of new Christian relationship there begins a gentle warning of the Holy Spirit, "Do not put your trust in man. Stay close to Me."

This believer continues to look to the pastor as a wonderful person given to them by God to fulfill all his spiritual needs (so far, so good). Then one day the usual fulfilling ministry does not flow. Oops. Not that they are offended, it is just that their expectation have not been met. A gap has manifest. Satan looks for these gaps. He

18

sows seeds of discord and tells the believer, "You deserve more; I mean after all, look at all you've done for this church." Sound familiar? We have all heard it at one time or another.

But what does such disappointment with our church life really indicate? Disappointment indicates misdirected desire. Our focus has shifted from a desire for a relationship with the Lord to a desire for relationship with the pastor. Besides, Pastor seems to meet our spiritual needs almost better than God does. Such a desire indicates a gap has formed in the relationship the believer has been developing with the Lord. Usually by this point corporate worship has replaced individual worship in his life.

ENTER THE ENEMY

Now the Enemy enters the picture with thoughts of rejection and dislike. Thoughts are the arrows he shoots through the gaps. Attacking the mind of the Christian, he will sow one of two lies. He will either give the believer a short list of reasons why he should no longer appreciate the pastor, or convince the believer the pastor no longer appreciates him. Either way, the results are the same; discord, strife, envy, etc.

The same set of circumstances gives rise to the alarming number of divorces among Christians. Rather than having Jesus as the source of fulfillment, couples look to each other. They develop certain expectations of each other and impose demands. When these are not fulfilled, the same Divider is there to sow the same kinds of thoughts. A couple with over twenty years in a wonderful marriage will tell you they have fallen "out of love" with each other. A gap has widened until it is a gaping hole through which the life of the marriage is being sucked out. The resulting devastation will effect generations.

If you can see the gaps in your life, the lives of others, the church, or your nation, it is because you are seeing from the vantage point of God's great love for His people and the world. Because you have that vision, God is calling you to get into that gap and to pray. God is allowing you to see things as He does so that through your prayers there can be agreement on the earth with His perfect plan for mankind.

What intercession really means is to intervene between parties with a view to reconciling differences. This is no great revelation; it is the definition of the word from Webster's Dictionary. But, part of the problem for the modern church is so many other things have been substituted for standing in the gap to effect that reconciliation. So often it is very instructive to see what something is not, in order to see what it is. After all, in wanting to be "gap standers" or intercessors we would certainly not want to be led...

DOWN THE GARDEN PATH

Have you ever seen this scenario? A sincere group of people decide they have been called to "Intercessory Ministry." They begin to meet as a small group, usually at a time which is not convenient for anyone else in the church. A general call is given to the church for prayer requests to be given to this "special group of intercessors" whom the Lord has "raised up."

After several months, the first directive suggestions begin to trickle out from the group. They feel that they have seen the will of God for the church and for individuals in it, particularly members of the leadership team. Soon they are talking to the younger singles about their life direction.

Given respect by the leadership and common courtesy by church members, they grow in intensity. Now they are aware of the "ruler spirits and strongholds" which are set against the church. These are rumored to have appeared to them in their prayer meetings. Often they claim to be aware of the spiritual forces which are operating in the lives of leadership. They become very spiritual in demeanor. They will not open their intensity or spirituality to question by those who are younger in the Lord or less experienced.

Now spiritual visitation becomes a part of their "prayer time." They do warfare against demonic forces which somehow never seem to totally lift from the church. They develop an image to accompany the word "intercession." It conveys an air of knowing more than anyone else in their church body...even the pastor.

Soon, they begin to "discern" spiritual activity in each other. They spend their prayer time "ministering" to each other. They focus on the enemy's attack on them because they are "prime intercessors." The inference is that if they who are so strong in the Lord are having these difficulties, how can mere believers survive. Those who hear about these things decide they will never be able to sustain a prayer ministry. They determine that they are far too weak for such warfare.

STAYING ON COURSE

I am not mocking the process of spiritual discernment, but this group, however well-intentioned at their beginning, have moved far away from true intercession. Their self-focus and self-orientation has culminated in spiritual pride, and taken them far off course. Paul warns us to **"Let no one cheat you of your reward, taking delight in false humility,..."** (Colossians 2:18a NKJV). It is this false humility through which the Enemy has begun to defeat this otherwise sincere group.

There is a phrase you will begin to hear from group members like these, which will tell you they are close to this point. They will say they are being called to a time of personal cleansing before they can handle any more prayer requests. They will begin to stress the importance of preparation of the intercessor over the Lord's ability to provide grace to cover their weaknesses.

Gosh, doesn't that sound spiritual? The problem is, it isn't correct.

It is understood in our walk with Jesus that we are not worthy to be included in His plans. That will never change. In fact, the celebration of our weakness opens our hearts for the worship of His excellence. Paul says, **"Most gladly therefore will I rather glory in my infirmities, that the power of Christ may rest upon me"** (2 Corinthians 12:9). He knew he could rejoice that the kingdom of God was not altered by the strength of his performance on any given day. This is no small concept; it is spiritual reality. We must have our heads on straight about this matter. It is vital to the flow of the power of the Holy Spirit in our lives.

FALLING INTO THE TRAP

Our group of would-be intercessors has fallen into the trap of "self perfection" to attain a throne room position with Christ. The problem is that the access to the throne of God is given through the blood of the Lamb, not by works of righteousness. The very best prayer and the very best works do not gain us access to grace. Grace is gained by one thing only, and that is the precious, all-powerful blood of Christ.

If you are part of a group like this, please ask yourself if this expression is becoming frequent among you. If it is, remind yourselves of the grace of God in calling you to ministry. Remind each other of your simple first love experience with Christ in prayer. Read Andrew Murray and Charles Finney on prayer. Work your way back to true humility which cries out to the Lord in utter amazement that I should even have a place in the plan of the Savior to be saved by His blood.

You and your group can be used in a mighty way when you hurdle the high place of humility. Get it settled in your spirit that the only worthy One is Christ. You are not going to arrive at any higher a pinnacle of perfection for you already have access to the throne room. Do not allow the Devil to tempt you with what you already have.

TEARING DOWN OUR OWN STRONGHOLDS

We receive clear caution in the Word that the strongholds we must tear down are those of our own minds.

> **Casting down imaginations, and every high
> thing that exalteth itself against the knowledge
> of God, and bringing into captivity every
> thought to the obedience of Christ;...**
> **2 Corinthians 10:5**

It is the imaginations, the inflated thoughts of self worth, which lift themselves against the knowledge of Christ. They must be brought under subjection to the truth. Your personal knowledge of Jesus Christ has lifted you to be a coworker with Him. You do not attain any higher position than the one you presently have. You are seated with Christ at the right hand of the Father. To attempt to pull yourself higher is to do exactly what Lucifer did.

> **For thou hast said in thine heart, I will ascend
> into heaven, I will exalt my throne above the
> stars of God:...I will ascend above the heights of
> the clouds; I will be like the most High.**
> **Isaiah 14:13,14**

We must be happy in the realization of what we have in Christ. This is why Paul prays for the Ephesians that the eyes of their understanding might be enlightened (Ephesians 1:18). When we realize all that Christ has given us, we cease from our own labors and enter into the rest which He has provided. His power through us causes even the demons to bow down.

Those who do not remind themselves daily of their weakness will finally come to their leadership with "direction from God" for the body. At this point they are no longer teachable; correction is out of the question. The pastoral team does not follow their input and division occurs. More than one church split has happened just this way. We had the same temptation in our ministry several years ago.

WORN THE SHOES—WALKED THE PATH

Many years ago, as a young pastor, I was amazed to see this process in operation. One day one of the group of "intercessors" burst into my office declaring she knew what direction the church should take with one of our families. Now, as a pastor, I was wondering how she had obtained such detailed information about one of our church families. I listened quite closely to her energetic call for me to discipline them.

I was more inclined to mercy. Somehow the thought of telling someone they could no longer be a part of the church was a little much for me. I felt that was far beyond my job description. As I appealed for mercy and longsuffering in the situation, I was rebuked as being typical of all pastoral leadership, that is, unable to take a stand for Christ. I refrained from pointing out that for years I had risked my life on the mission fields of the world.

As the lady left in the same haste with which she had entered, I reflected on a few things. God's mercy exceeds His wrath. He is longsuffering with us all, and thank God for it. He adds to the church daily as He sees fit. Jesus said He would build the church and cautioned strongly against offending any one of His sheep.

I chose mercy.

That same prayer group happened to be holding a

retreat for women over the next weekend, and I made a point to see her again. The following Monday she appeared at my door in quite a state of excitement. She told me about the glorious time they had at the retreat, and I was impressed with what I saw as a certain change about her. Then she gave me the news.

"You should have seen God move," she said. "He led us to cast the lying spirits out of each other." She was thrilled.

I couldn't help it. I had to ask the obvious question. "If a lying spirit had been cast out of you, then it's a good thing we didn't do as you had suggested last week, isn't it?" Her enthusiasm dampened a little bit.

When she left my office I was deeply troubled. How had this happened in our church? These were very nice people. They had formed the group with all good intentions to intercede. I feel to this day they were very sincere and had only good motives in what they were doing, but what had happened?

TRUE INTERCESSION

The second letter in our **W-I-N** acrostic is **I** and it stands for intercession...true intercession.

The problem was this group had never known or completely understood the true definition of intercession. They had their own idea of the call to intercessory prayer, but had not gained a biblical understanding of what intercession really is. Rather than being instruments for reconciling differences, they had become instruments for division, questioning leaders and stumbling babes. They had gotten out of the gap and had begun to lord a false spirituality over the flock.

I thank God He did intervene in our lives. Today they continue to meet and to seek His face. I have no doubt that as the Holy Spirit leads them, they pray for me and I thank God for that. But in those years, we all had many lessons to learn. Our zeal was beyond question, but we had very little experience.

A healthy ministry of intercession reaches out to and includes people. Exclusivity is the enemy of God's purpose. If every man, woman, and child on this planet is going to have the opportunity to receive Jesus Christ as Lord and Savior, we must include people in prayer rather than exclude them.

While intercession can include a lot of things, e.g. worship, prayer, prophetic acts, etc., one thing it must include is intervention. To "intervene" in this case is like playing the role of referee in a boxing match. He is irrelevant until he is needed; then he steps between the combatants and sets things in motion correctly again.

How do you like irrelevance? Very few people do. That is why so many folks doing the work of God declare themselves to be a "ministry." They are not content to just disappear from the mainstream and seek the Lord. It is in the heart of man to have a title. We are conditioned by the world's system to look out for number one. To take care of ourselves. To promote ourselves. To make sure we save face in every circumstance.

We want our labor to be for something significant. Does it bother you when people say, "All we can do now is pray." Or, "I guess we'll just have to trust the Lord on this one." Who else **would** you trust? And why wait till the bitter end to pray? Men ought always to pray (1 Thessalonians 5:17). Ephesians 6:18 goes a step further encouraging us to pray always in the Spirit.

Indeed our work in the Lord is in vain if we fail to pray. Jesus spent night and day in prayer. He said, **"...The Son can do nothing of himself, but what he seeth the Father do: for what things soever he doeth, these also doeth the Son likewise"** (John 5:19). How do you suppose He gained such insight? He walked among man in continual communication with the Father. That is prayer walking.

Have you ever wondered how Jesus managed to spend so much time among people and they still didn't know who He was? He made himself of no reputation. He did not have an advance team; at least not one you could see. He was a study in avoiding the ways of man for He had a heavenly vision: to effect the perfect will of God in His life and the lives of those with whom He came in contact. What is the perfect will of God? That every man, woman and child have the opportunity to hear the Gospel in a way they can understand it. The result: He attained the highest reputation ever afforded anyone in all of recorded history.

JESUS IN THE GAP

In 1983 I was trekking in Nepal. At that time it was illegal to change religion in that beautiful land. The jail terms were one year for converting, three years for leading someone to the Lord, and six years per person for water baptism.

We were trekking from village to village, distributing Christian literature and praying for the sick. The previous day we had handed out about two hundred tracts and the response had been very great. Now we walked into the town of Gaighat, Sagamatha Province. This very busy village was Panchat, a sort of county seat.

We entered the place in the heat of the day and stopped to rest on a low stone wall adjacent to the local school. The children were attracted to the two very different-looking Westerners. They ran over to see us and were very curious about what might be in our rattan baskets. Our porters, also weary from the journey, were looking forward to spending the night in this town and had left us there on the wall to fend for ourselves, while they went to make arrangements. The crowd of children grew and two of the braver boys, perhaps ten years of age, began to open the baskets. We let them.

BUSTED

Across the way from us was a man in legal garb. Attorneys in Nepal have a very distinctive haircut and robe. This was obviously a man of some legal influence. As the children began to open the baskets and shout with joy at the books they found, this man turned and hastily headed toward the police station.

Calling to the porters, I expressed my concern, but they were not inclined to move quickly. So we Westerners took off as fast as we could go and left them behind. We were certain there was going to be a problem. We were right.

As the oldest and heaviest of our team, I was the one the police caught up with first. The arrest was very professional, but the arresting officer did tell me I was in a lot of trouble. The Chief District Officer had ordered my arrest for preaching Christianity through the books we carried. The officer was under orders to stop my flight and to bring me at once before the CDO.

As I walked back down the trail to face certain difficulty, the Lord spoke to me, "If you deny Me before man, I will deny you before the Father."

The voice was as clear as day. The certainty of its tenor gripped my heart so that minutes later when the CDO asked, "Are you a Christian?" it was very easy to say, "Yes." When he further asked, "Are you a baptized Christian?" It was even easier to say, "Yes, sir, I have been baptized three times," (once as a child, once as an adult believer, and once in the Holy Spirit).

"I LIVE TO MAKE INTERCESSION FOR YOU"

As I said that, the same voice spoke to me saying, "I live to make intercession for you." It was so real. No one else in the room heard it. The CDO never heard it. But

28

there was Jesus telling me He had the situation under control. He was standing in a major gap in my life that day. He was drawing together these events and the perfect plan of the Father.

After lengthy dialogue in which I shared the message of the Gospel with the CDO, he decided to let me go, along with our team. His exact words were, "I have decided to show you grace." Where did a Hindu official come up with the word "grace?" God was speaking through him. Instead of six hundred years in jail, I was going on with the rest of our scheduled trek.

Six months later, that same man walked out of his office and from a clear blue sky was struck dead by lightening. It was reported in the Katmandu paper and the Christian brothers in Nepal saved the clipping for me. For years I thought about that lightning strike as retribution; you know, **"Touch not mine anointed, and do my prophets no harm"** (1 Chronicles 16:22). But one morning the Lord corrected me. "Rather," He suggested, "see how much it took for Me to get a pampered, self-centered, Christian preacher (that would be me, in case you hadn't guessed) over to Nepal to share the faith with that man, knowing he had just six months to live."

You see, Jesus was in the gap for **him**, too. The CDO neither knew Him nor knew where to find Him, but had a need to know Him. God orchestrated the arrest, used the Nepali attorney and even my size to bring us to the gap. Jesus was busy interceding and indeed, I have never been better cared for. The plan of man was made to conform to the plan of God, and the intercessor was unseen throughout.

FIRST BLOOD

Philippians 2 teaches us that Jesus made Himself of no reputation and served us in the great gap of Gethsemane. The blood of the covenant was first shed there. Not Pilate, not the high priest, not the Devil extracted the first drops of that cleansing flow. They dropped as sweat from His body in the agony of intercession. The blood began to flow in a place where no one else could see it. Intercession is a private matter.

Yet, intercession is so powerful that all the sin of man can be washed away by it. God was in Christ reconciling man to himself. He was in Gethsemane as the Intercessor for you. Yes, the plan of man was made to conform to the plan of God that every man, woman, and child on the earth would have the opportunity to know Jesus as their Lord and Savior. Jesus prayed that for you in that garden. He lifted you before the Father before you were born.

He paid the price and now He has the greatest reputation. He has defeated the Devil above the earth, on the earth, and under the earth. He has risen far above every power and principality. He has opened the gates of heaven and now **lives** in the gap for you (Hebrews 7:25). You have an Advocate with the Father. Go ahead and thank Him!

IT WORKS FOR YOU TOO

You do not have to be preoccupied with how you are doing. The One who can open the seals has taken up His position as intercessor for you. Receive that gift with thanksgiving and be happy for He lives to intercede for you. You are the object of His love. He looks upon you with delight as He sees His own prayers answered daily in your life. You are a joy to Him. You are accepted in the beloved. Jesus loves you. Jesus accepts you. As a born-again believer, you are just as if you have never sinned in His sight.

When you have that locked into your spirit and your relationship with Him is secure, you are ready to step into the gap for others. You will be able to appear as an irrelevant or extraneous feature without it bothering you. You will have exchanged the desire for prominence for the desire to be significant. You'll know the event is not about you. You'll know you were called there to pray, not posture, not parade, not even to preach.

Step into that gap. Intervene. Take up that position of humility that declares your weakness and the Lord's strength. Appeal to God's ultimate purpose on someone else's behalf. You are in the gap as a result of your relationship with Jesus, just as He is in the gap for you as a result of His relationship with His Father.

CHAPTER 3

Abraham, Our Example

A braham was a family man. When God instructed him to leave his family and separate himself to God's purpose, he took along his nephew Lot. We have no idea what agreements were made amongst the members of the family, but we do know the patriarch was, or felt he was, responsible for Lot.

Abraham was obedient, coming to rest in a place of peace called the plains of Mamre, when the Lord came by (Genesis 18). Remember the Spirit of the Lord is moving in all the earth looking for those through whom He can be glorified. Abraham had put himself in the gap, albeit unknowingly, and God found him. How did he place himself in the gap, you ask?

Abraham worshiped. That is, he got up from his rest and beckoned to the Lord to come and fellowship with him. Abraham made himself available to God. He called to Him. What an example! All successful Christian endeavor comes from an attitude of worship. He got up from the place of peace where he was content and called upon the Lord for a time of fellowship. When worship moves into fellowship you have stepped into the gap.

God and Abraham had a meal together. The blood of the calf of sacrifice speaks of acceptance in the beloved because of their existing covenant. The bread and wine speak of the new covenant which is to come in Jesus. Abraham had relationship with God. The "Father of Faith" and the "Father of the Spirit" ate together. The purpose of man is about to conform to the purpose of God.

THE AFTER DINNER WALK

After dinner, the Lord excused Himself and headed on down the road. Abraham followed the Eastern custom and saw his Guest off in proper fashion. They walked together for a while and the Lord was mindful of Scripture He would be inspiring a couple thousand years later, **"He will do nothing without first telling His servants the prophets"** (Amos 3:7 author's paraphrase). He thought for awhile about the man with whom He was walking and the reason for His journey. *"Abraham is a just man and is going to serve me all his days,"* the Lord thought. *"Is it right for me to do something without telling him?"*

Have you ever wondered what God is thinking about as you linger in His presence? So often we sing a few songs and then rush on to the announcements or the day's schedule or program. This text tells us God is thinking about us in covenant terms. He is making a decision. In this case He is determining the present from His knowledge of the future. He relates to you not according to what you have been, but according to what you shall be.

He shares His mission with Abraham. God is going to purge the people of Sodom of sin and its consequences, perhaps even AIDS. That's right. Sodom and Gomorrah are homosexual communities. How do we know that? From Genesis 19:5. The men of the city wanted to have sexual relations with the angels for they were fair to look upon. Where did you think the term *sodomy* came from?

When God tells Abraham His plan to destroy Sodom, Abraham appeals for the life of Lot, his nephew who is living there. Abraham and God dialogue as they walk. This is prayer walking. Abraham finally steps in front of God. Talk about standing in the gap for someone! He beseeches God to spare the city for the sake of its righteous people. First, he asks that the city be spared if there are fifty righteous people. God agrees. Abraham reduces the number and asks again. Again, God agrees. Abraham continues reducing the number and asking until finally he stops at ten righteous people. But there aren't even ten. Still, God's mercy exceeds His wrath, so He spares those who call upon Him and destroys the rest. What a message for today. He spares those who call upon Him and destroys the rest.

Of course, Lot has to leave all that is associated with living in Sodom. But his wife cannot separate from her love for those things or the city and turns as if to return. She is turned to a pillar of salt. The entire region is barren to this day. Whatever virus was there was terminated.

Abraham stood in the gap for Lot and his family, and did so boldly. We can do the same for our families, and do it just as boldly because we operate under a better covenant with better promises.

INTERCESSORS TODAY

I hear politicians and "do gooders," and the media is filled with issues and non-answers. But where are the intercessors? They are walking with God. They appear as irrelevant or extraneous. They are not on TV; they are not included at the summits on AIDs, and they are scorned if they say anything. Eventually, when the way of man has run its course, the problem will be brought to the feet of Christ. At that time, one of those whom the world thought was homophobic will have divine wisdom and God's mercy will be made manifest.

Exodus 32 and 33 are a study on developing an intercessory relationship. As we join the action in verse 30, the people have sinned a great sin. Moses, as their leader, has to take a course of action. He steps into the gap. He returns to the Lord.

Can you imagine saying to a teenager caught cheating in school, "I am going to go and see if I can make atonement for you?" To make atonement means to make up for some error or deficiency; in the extreme it means to give your life as payment.

In other words, Moses is saying he is going to go before God in the place of the guilty to plead for them. The innocent sacrificing himself for the guilty! Will you give yourself to a life of prayer? Will you be a Moses standing before God? Will you be an Abraham standing in God's way bargaining for the life another?

In Exodus 32:32 Moses makes an extraordinary request. He has so identified with the people he is willing to bear the consequence of their sin. He gives God a choice: forgive their sin or blot his own name out of the book of life.

The Lord's response is that sin and its consequence are a personal matter. Each person must bear the consequence of his own sin. Further, the context tells us that, while they were subsequently led through the wilderness by the Angel of the Lord, Israel was still plagued because of the golden calf they had made to worship in Exodus 32:35.

GOD'S SOLUTION—PRAYER WALKING

In spite of Israel's failings, God makes a great commitment to Moses in the next few sentences. He says He will come along on the trip. He is going to walk in the midst of the people to prevent the spoken plague from destroying them before they arrive at His promise. He describes them as a stiff-necked people. As such, they will always have a gap between them and God, but since He loves them, in response to Moses' plea, He will close the gap.

When told this news, the people are sad. Not that they are going to get the promise, but that God is in their midst because they are stiff-necked. Is this a great gap? You are in one about the same size. You tell your loved ones Jesus wants to walk with them and, instead of being happy, they are sad. You tell your young folks if they will walk with the Lord they will be blessed and, instead of going for the promise, they are sad about the condition.

It was the same for Isaiah and for Jesus. You remember that Isaiah was going to be rejected, by ninety percent of the people (Isaiah 6:9). Jesus was despised and rejected a man of sorrows and acquainted with grief (Isaiah 53:3). He was eventually abandoned to the cross by even His best friends on earth. But there in Gethsemane, when even the closest could not fellowship with Him in prayer, He was met by the Father and the angels ministered to Him. He was sustained by that heavenly vision.

THE KEY TO SUCCESS AS AN INTERCESSOR

God establishes relationship with the intercessor. The people go out of the camp to find God in the tabernacle and nothing happens. Moses goes to the same place and the glory of God manifests as the two friends discuss the pressures of leading six million stubborn people in a way they have never gone.

God meets Moses in the gap. This causes all of the people to turn their attention toward that tent. They had not seen the presence of God before now. They had seen His power against Egypt. They had covered their door posts against His wrath, but they had not seen His glory. As Moses and God fellowship in the tabernacle, the cloudy pillar appears to the people and they do what the Lord has placed in their hearts. They worship. **All successful Christian endeavor comes from an attitude of worship.** The people only wanted to see God's ways; Moses wanted

His presence!

Moses leaves the tabernacle of intercession to return to his role of leadership. The people now honor him because he met with God face to face. One young man remains in the tabernacle. He is learning the lessons of the presence of God which will enable him to lead the next generation of these people. He is communing with the Person of God who will one day meet him before the closed gate of Jericho and instruct him in how to take the land. He is Joshua.

The hours of worship in the tabernacle gave Joshua great faith. He was ready to receive the promise God had given for he had spent time in fellowship with the One whose word is true. In Numbers 14 this confidence causes him to proclaim to the people the Lord will give them the land as He has promised. Indeed, it is Joshua who contends with the people for the promise.

AN UNHAPPY PEOPLE

Yet the people are not happy with Moses. In fact, they take up stones to kill him. Why is it that the one who seeks God and appeals to faith is always the target for the stones of those who rebel? Could it be that the offended ones are also trying to fill the gap? Do they sense the distance? Has the peaceful presence and powerful purpose of God become distant to them as well?

God's response is He will disinherit them, He will destroy them, He will make a new and mightier nation who will enter in (Numbers 14:12). For the moment, Moses is the only one who can stand in the gap. He does not appeal to the Lord's nature of longsuffering. He does not call out for protection for himself or his young leaders. Instead, he appeals to God's ultimate purpose.

THE APPEAL TO ULTIMATE PURPOSE

He reminds the Lord that should God destroy this people, the nations will have no reason to believe His promises either (vs. 15). It is the will of God that every man, women, and child on the earth hear the Gospel in a way they can understand. So to destroy the people called by His name would defeat His own purpose. How many years of solitary intercession and relationship building do you think it took for Moses to understand the impact on the heart of God his counsel would have?

Do you intercede according to the ultimate plan of God? Are you asking Him to fulfill His plan or yours? We know if we ask anything according to His will he hears us and grants the petition we desire of Him (1 John 5:14-15). If you are living your life to fulfill His purpose, that every man woman and child would have the opportunity to receive Jesus in your generation, then ask Him to remember the promise of all things that pertain to life and godliness, ask on in confidence.

Moses' appeal to ultimate purpose released pardon and the declaration that the glory of the Lord will fill all the earth (Numbers 14:20-21). Because there was an intercessor in the gap, the plan of God did not stop with a rebellious and stiff-necked people, but continued on to the next generation.

Caleb is selected as the "seed bearer" to the promised land. Caleb was selected for two reasons. First, he was not of the same spirit as the others, he was the elder of the tribe of Judah hence baring the title, "The Lion of the tribe of Judah." Not only did he have the title and the anointing, secondly, he was also obedient. He followed the Lord fully.

THE PURPOSE OF THE WILDERNESS EXPERIENCE

Those who did not obey the Lord were led into a wilderness designed for death. The function of the Old Testament wilderness was to see the death of the previous generation and the training of the subsequent. It is the same in our wilderness experience. Death of the old, preparation of the new. Moses stood in the gap for those who would die. Even though they had caused so many problems for him, we see in Deuteronomy 9:25-29 his heart of prayer for them.

He first mentions he has fasted and prayed for them for forty days. Wow, what a gap! Imagine having to fast for forty days before receiving the assurance God was going to hear your prayer. Can you imagine how many times in those six weeks without food he wanted to say, "OK, God, blast them!"

Moses' motive had been God's declaration of destruction of the nation. Can you grasp the fear of God this man had to believe Him so strongly that food was set aside and faith took its place? He is not praying to an extension of his father image. He is not gazing through crystals or burning incense to a rock that cannot speak. Moses is talking to the true and living God who has dramatically demonstrated His awesome power.

They had met at a bush, walked the deserts together, faced Pharaoh, and parted the Red Sea. Moses had seen the hand of God in deliverance and destruction. There was no doubt the Power with whom he spoke could do whatever He desired.

ULTIMATE PURPOSE AGAIN

Moses reminds God of His love for the people, the fact that He had chosen them. He makes strong point of all the Lord has done for these people in bringing them out of Egypt. He asks God not to consider the nature of these who had groaned in Egypt but as the Lord of Abraham, Isaac, and Jacob, to remember those whose lives God had chosen to bear His own name among men. For, he concludes, God is the God of the living, not the dead.

Then he appeals to God's ultimate purpose, "You do not want the nations to reject You by saying You could not do what You said You would do" (Deuteronomy 9:28). This is powerful prayer. It is the character of God which is shown forth in His actions. Moses realizes the Devil is waiting to see the outcome of the rebellion of Israel.

Satan has his heralds, the kings of the nations, ready to shout the news throughout the earth that the mighty God who threw him out of heaven has been defeated by the fear in His own people; that God made a mistake in choosing man. The kings of the nations are under his deceiving power to attack those chosen vessels of the Seed of Abraham.

Would God abandon His promise to His friend? Will He abandon you when you are stubborn and rebellious? The Enemy would love to tell you that God is ashamed of you. That your salvation is not valid for the day-to-day failures in your life. He will try to get you to believe, instead of standing in the gap for others, you are a such a mess yourself you should have an army of intercessors standing in the gap for you.

How did Moses quiet all of these thoughts? The same way Jesus did, he fasted. He took away the enemy's device of lust and appetite. His appetite was for the Lord.

In the power of position in God's gap, Moses prayed according to the word of God. "You have said you will bring them out," He reminds the Lord. It is the character of God to fulfill His promises to man. Therefore He will have to change His nature to destroy the people at this point. Moses has used a powerful tool of intercession: prayer according to the word of the Lord.

IT'S YOUR TURN NOW

Now, have you seen some new gaps? How about those family members? Can you think of a teen who needs your prayers? How about the life of your church? Is the worship in the heavenlies? Is the preacher in the Word? How about those people on your TV who are so obviously unreached?

Take a few moments right now and intercede for one of the gaps you are aware of. We'll still be here when you come back. Pray. Step into that gap. Intervene. Take up the position of humility which declares your weakness and the Lord's strength. Pray according to the plan of God. Appeal to His ultimate purpose that every man woman and child know His Son. Agree with God for a while, we will wait here for you.

Let the Lord form a prayer list for you. Get paper and a pen and let Him lead you from name to name. Write them down with today's date and get ready to hear the answer. God is not slack concerning His promises (2 Peter 3:9). Go ahead, give yourself to it and you will find yourself in the place of success for an intercessor: the presence of God Himself.

CHAPTER 4
Neutralize The Enemy

My early days as a missionary were spent in the wonderful country of Guatemala. In those days Guatemala was recovering from the earthquake of 1976. God had used the quake to open the doors for evangelical and charismatic ministries to flood the land with the good news of Jesus. Following on the heels of a century of missions work, this army of soul gatherers found great success, a tribute to the seed which had been sown there.

For my part, the Lord had given me a burden for small villages in what we called the "marginal" areas. These were settlements which had sprung up around the capital as people came in search of a better life. In the course of working among these people I became intrigued with the villages from which they had come, and after a couple of years found myself walking among those villages with a small day bag stuffed with Spanish bibles.

I would drive each day to road's end and then walk the footpaths looking for someone who could read Spanish. When I found a reader I would give them a Bible and a reading assignment with the agreement that they would read the assignment to those in the family who could not read. Each week I would return, answer questions, and give the next assignment.

Often the oldest child in a family was the only one who could read, and the proud father would assure me he would gather the rest of the family each day to hear from the Book.

In this simple way we found success in reaching many villages with the word of God. Good news spreads fast and soon there were house groups, and churches were beginning to organize. People were waiting for me on the appointed days to claim a Bible for their family. In natural progression, there were healings and salvations and baptisms and churches formed.

It seemed too good to last and, of course, it did not go unchallenged by the Devil.

THE MASTER'S STRATEGY

One morning as I went out to the villages, I was blessed to have the company of a precious brother, Gilbert Dilley. Gilbert and his family had moved from Indiana to work in the reconstruction and he was pastoring those of us who had formed a Sunday night fellowship in English. He was interested to see how our ministry was coming.

We arrived in the town of San Jose del Golfo and were joined by the elder there, Lazuro Ochoa Catalan, and two policemen. One of the police was a new brother in the church. He delivered the news to me that I was not going out to the villages as there was a very important meeting awaiting our arrival. I mildly suggested I had to go because the people would be waiting, and it wasn't right to disappoint them. He firmly assured me I was not going but would attend this meeting.

San Jose is the municipal center of government for

about thirty small villages extending from the Atlantic Coast Highway to the Motagua River just fifteen miles east of Guatemala City. The Lord had given us small groups in each of the villages and a church in San Jose. Our influence was building in the area and had caught the attention of the government.

As we entered the large meeting room of the town hall, I recognized most of the men. The mayor of San Jose was there as well as the sub-mayors who presided over each community where I had been distributing bibles. They were easily distinguished by their hats and official sticks.

The mayor greeted me and thanked me for being there. He wanted to know who Gilbert was and said Lazuro did not have to stay but could if he wanted to. Two of the closest friends I will ever know, both men said they would be glad to stay.

The mayor explained that this was a special and very important meeting because these men wanted me to declare my intention in their communities. When I asked him exactly how important, he said it would be the most important meeting I would probably ever attend.

CALLED TO ORDER

Calling the meeting to order, the mayor had each man stand in front of a chair all of which formed a circle. He explained to the men who I was, although most of them knew me. He took great pains to formally introduce Gilbert and Lazuro and expressed their desire to remain. He explained my Spanish was fine so there was no need for translation. I would understand their questions and could answer quite well.

While all this was going on I was in the Spirit quietly asking God to neutralize the power of the Enemy arrayed against us so His work could go on to bear fruit.

When the mayor suggested we start with questions,

I immediately jumped in with what the Lord had given me, not knowing where it would lead or even what the next step would be.

"I realize this is a very important meeting and I want to express my appreciation for you coming all the way to be here. May I suggest, since this is such an important meeting, we follow a custom which we have in my country for such occasions."

They thought that was a good idea and so I explained to them, "In meetings of this importance in my country, we always start with prayer."

They looked at each other and again at me. They were not men of prayer.

"Since this is such an important meeting," I continued to cover their hesitation, "it is important the prayer be done properly. Just custom you understand."

They were getting a little upset with the length of time this was taking, but they were going along with it, just to be customarily correct.

"Now in prayers like this it is customary for us as men to pray with our hats off."

They looked to the mayor who, with a condescending shrug, removed his hat. They too removed their hats and looked around at each other. I cannot recall another meeting in Latin America in which all men had their hats off.

NERVOUS OBEDIENCE

Now I was nervous, but I continued as the Lord gave me instructions.

"Since this is such an important meeting, and we surely wanted it to go well, perhaps we should follow custom another step."

The mayor was not smiling when his eye caught mine. I had pushed this about as far as I was going to be able.

"Perhaps," I suggested, "we should join hands to pray."

Latin men do not stand around with their hats off holding hands. They looked to the mayor and then to me; you could see the fire in their eyes. I took the hands of Gilbert and Lazuro and they in turn reached out for the others. The men placed their hats and sticks on the chairs behind them and took hands. A nervous laughter went through the place.

Now, feeling very hung out there by the Lord, I said, "I know that many of you are not used to praying and since this has to be right, may I suggest I lead you in prayer and you all repeat the prayer after me."

Somewhat relieved, they were quick to agree.

"Lord Jesus," I began, and they followed. "Forgive me of my sins. Come into my life as my personal Savior and Lord. Give me the power to be a good man and a good leader for my people, in Jesus name."

EARTH SHAKING EXPERIENCE

When they said "in Jesus name," the earth literally shook! There was an earthquake. The place shook violently from side to side as well as up and down. I was scared to death. Holding Gilbert and Lazuro's hands tight, I did not open my eyes.

The quake measured 6.5 we found out later. The mayors ran from the building as they were afraid the terra cotta tiles would come crashing down through the wooden rafters and crush our skulls. Taking no thought for important hats or sticks, they dashed from the building.

Now, when a tremor stops, there is a complete silence. Dogs do not bark, birds do not chirp, all creation stands still waiting to see if it is going to happen again. As the dust cleared around us, we three stood petrified by the impact of what had happened!

One by one the men reentered the room, found their hats and sticks, nodded to us and went off to find out the condition of their village. Finally, the head mayor came back in. He put on his hat and drawing himself to full stature he said, "I do not now how you did that; but I am authorized to tell you that whatever you need in any of these villages, you have only to ask the man who was in this room and he will get it for you. You are to come tomorrow with your passport and those of your family and friends and you will receive courtesy visas. From this day forward you are the invited guests of the government of Guatemala, you have no need to stop for immigration or customs, and should the national police stop you for any reason just show them this seal and you will be conducted safely and speedily to your destination."

Satan had not only been neutralized, his attack had been turned against him.

WE WIN!

The third letter in our acrostic **W-I-N** is **N** for **neutralize**.

I want to tell you, God will literally move heaven and earth to achieve His ultimate purpose. He wants every man woman and child on this planet to hear the message of His Son in a way they can understand. He wants you to stand in the gap, to enter into key locations in your city, country, and around this globe to call upon His name and see His power manifest.

He is the God of Acts chapter four, He is the God of Abraham, Isaac, and Jacob who changes not. He is the One to whom you are talking when you pray. It is He who has saved you and it is He who is calling you to pray.

Just as He will dwell above the blood on the mercy seat, between the angels, He will dwell above your life and His glory will be seen through you. The irresistible power of the love of Jesus will flow through you and thirty villages full of souls will be released by the power of God. All you have to do is enter in. Get into the gaps in your town and wait upon the Lord. Let the Enemy work his plan because it is going to be to your and the Lord's advantage.

Let them capture the ark if need be so the glory can be carried to the nations.

WE HAVE THE SOLUTION

Through the fall of man, Satan gained an advantage in the earth. This is universally accepted. From the temples of Buddhism to the halls of great governments, this fact of the fall of man is testified to. We have the only solution to neutralize the power of the Devil. The disciples reported the demons were subject to them in the name of Jesus (Luke 10:17). These first followers of Christ testified His name was above all names.

As we enter the gap, as we stand between the place of the Enemy and the lives of the people, we are used of God to neutralize the power of the Devil. I suggest you make a weekly trip to the campus of your son or daughter. If you don't have family, think about those young people whom you observe in the community. Go to that school and walk around it. Quietly declare the name of Jesus. Go with the intent of intercession. Don't make a big show, but do pray. Stand in that gap once a week and pray. Watch the news, watch the neighbors, watch your kids, you will hear the good report as you continue to pray.

Get four friends and cover the school week. Each one take a day. Just go the one hour and walk around or stand quietly somewhere and observe and pray. The Lord will give you the place as the power of the Devil is neutralized!!

There is no better place to be! **W-I-N** ...We win. Shout it!

Worship...

Intercede...

Neutralize the Enemy.. in your family, in your town, in your state, in your nation, around the world!

W...I...N WE WIN!

CHAPTER 5
The Fourfold Foundation

T his will be the shortest chapter in the book, but one of the most important. I've set it apart so it will be a clear path for you to follow in your own prayer life as you intercede for those you love and those God has called you to intercede for.

How is that prayer list of yours doing? Mine lists the names of family members and heads of state, Christian workers and their families. One of the things I like to do is put up pictures of people in my prayer room and just look around and pray for each one. Yes, you can send me one and I'll put you up there with the rest. I'm not promising you letters, and please do not send money for the prayers, but I will pray for you.

On the subject of prayer habits, let me share with you something Dick Eastman of Every Home for Christ taught me a long time ago. It is a habit of prayer which is according to the Word of God and has proven to be wonderful for me. It is found in detail in the Appendix A of his great book, *The Hour That Changes the World*.

There are four areas of prayer which Dick suggests.

I have made them the foundation of my prayer time. They make a great structure on which to build an hour of prayer. It was these four which sustained me during years of prayer for changes in the Soviet Union.

First, we pray for **Workers.** Jesus said we were to pray the Lord of the harvest that He would send laborers into the harvest (Luke 10:2). As I walk the nations of the earth and pray for the souls of the people, my constant cry is for workers. The harvest is ready. We need workers. Not just from our country, but nationals as well. Not just eager beavers, but trained harvesters.

Second, we pray for **Open Doors.** Paul said it this way, **"[Pray]...that God would open unto us a door of utterance,"** (Colossians 4:3). There is no such thing as a closed door to a praying person. Because we are in touch with a heavenly vision and a spiritual kingdom, we can see beyond the limitations of negativism and the present situation. The Russians used to tell us "Nyet" when we would try to witness, bring Bibles, hand out tracts, sing Christian songs, or fellowship with Soviet Christians. We heard it as, "Not yet."

Each time we were rebuffed we would reassure ourselves by saying that we were one day closer to the opening. We would ride the Trans-Siberian Railway and speak revival to the countryside. We would get down for a couple days in major cities and walk about in them calling upon the Lord to drive out the darkness to open the door.

During those years I often said that communism would fall and the Gospel would be preached throughout Europe. I was rebuked many times by people who had to have communism to fulfil their end-time plan. We just kept praying, "Open the door." How we rejoice today as so many souls have entered in to praise the Lord, and volumes of testimony have been written about the churches in those cities.

Third, we pray for **Fruit.** Jesus told the disciples in the upper room that He would pray the Father would give them fruit for their labors. We call forth the fruit of righteousness when we pray. We speak fruitfulness to your ministry. Fruitfulness means souls are saved and prayers are answered. Jesus will give us the fruit of our labors because it comes from the vine and not the branches. He is the vine, we are the branches. Your fruit is His fruit.

Fourth, we pray for **Finances.** Actually, we pray for the entire material realm. I do not want to own a Boeing 747. I have no place to put it. But, I do need a seat on one fairly often. As we pray the hour of prayer, we loose full provision for the Church so our workers can go through open doors and bring forth much fruit. The Lord does answer prayers.

Often I am asked about our funding strategy. My answer is the condition of my knees and one fourth of my prayer life. Jesus had no gimmicks in His earthly ministry, and we don't need to use any in conducting His ministry now. He not only provides, He is the both the Provider and the Provision. His command contains His provision. He said, "Ask," and so we do.

That's all. May I suggest you memorize this fourfold foundation for prayer? When you don't know what to pray for, this will get you started.

CHAPTER 6
Sing Your Song

My second son Matthew changed schools in the sixth grade. We had just returned from Asia and he was quite used to the Asian custom of singing in school. His new school did not have this custom and he had a difficult time understanding why it didn't. At first he thought he was the "odd ball," but one day he came bouncing home with the declaration that he had figured it out.

"The reason they don't sing," he reported, "is they don't have anything to sing about. They don't know about Jesus."

Matthew saw his purpose as sharing with his classmates the joy of Jesus. But he didn't do it in the flesh. Spiritual work must be done in a spiritual way. We began to walk our dog around the school each day. The dog needed the exercise and it gave us the chance to "spy out the land," and claim the school and the kids for the Lord. You know the end, of course, the Lord is faithful and many of the faculty and children have a song today.

Spiritual warfare is just that simple. In the sincere

attempt to convey the tremendous importance of intercession and spiritual warfare, many have complicated this
valuable ministry to an unattainable level. In this section
we are going to experience the joy of a very simple acrostic, **S.I.N.G.** It is the key to becoming an Attack Lamb.

It stands for:
Spy out the land
Interceding
Use The Name
Cut the Grass

SPY OUT THE LAND

In Matthew 10 Jesus commissions His twelve disciples. Come with me to that point and let's together observe the way in which He accomplishes this very important task. To find the flow of action, let's back up to the
last two verses of chapter nine, verses 37 and 38:

> **Then saith he unto His disciples, The harvest
> truly is plenteous, but the labourers are few; pray
> ye therefore the Lord of the harvest, that he will
> send forth labourers into His harvest.**

What a strategy! When I saw it, I was astounded at
its subtle simplicity.

Jesus is asking his disciples, and us, to pray according to His ultimate purpose; that every man woman and
child on the face of the earth have the opportunity to receive Him as their personal Lord and Savior. He is asking
each of us to pray for workers. Yet, He is the Lord of the
harvest, He is the One who owns the harvest, He is the
One who will send the harvesters, and yet He commands
our participation in prayer.

We have an important position! He has commanded you to pray that He will send forth the laborers.

Why is He doing that? Because He wants to include you in the powerful stream of His ultimate purpose.

See what happens next. The Lord calls to Himself those very ones whom He had commanded to pray. By virtue of their praying for laborers they have placed themselves in the gap of intercession and in a position to be called themselves into His purpose. Now, with His call, they become the answers to their own prayers!

Since I saw this powerful truth, I no longer ask people to come to the mission field. I just ask them to pray that someone will hear the call and join us in the flood of God's purpose. As their trickle of faith receives a deluge of power through the Holy Spirit, they join the flow which is flooding the globe with the good news of Jesus Christ.

Do you need workers for children's ministry? Do you need men with a heart to labor to add that education wing? Do you need volunteers to deliver meals or to sidewalk counsel? Don't put people on the spot, instead, ask them to pray that someone will come forward to do it. They will respond to God's call for they are being, through prayer, included in His ultimate purpose.

ATTACK LAMBS

Jesus said, **"Behold, I send you forth as sheep in the midst of wolves: be ye therefore wise as serpents, and harmless as doves"** (Matthew 10:16). Did he call you a sheep? No! You are no more a sheep than the Holy Spirit is a bird! He said you are "as a sheep." You are after the fashion of a sheep. Big difference!

Just think about this. You are out there as a sheep. The wolf sees you. "How 'bout a lamb chop for dinner?" he says to himself.

You can feel him sneaking up on you. Do you know what that feels like? I get a little queeze in the stomach. Or else I get what my sons call the "willies". At any rate, there are wolves around.

Maybe there are places you pass by on your way home from work or school where you feel this discerning chill. The radar goes off and your wolf alarm sounds. How about a particular boss or teacher? Have any that make you want to cry out, "I rebuke you in Jesus' name!"

There are wolves in the area. They sneak up on the sheep and pounce. They sink their claws in from behind. They grab that wool and tear it back. Dinner is served! Or so they think.

But wait! The wool comes off too easily. The wolf has been fooled. Something else is inside this sheepskin. It is a LION! It is the Lion of the tribe of Judah. **"...greater is he that is in you than he that is in the world"** (1 John 4:4). You are not a sheep at all! You are the temple of the Holy Ghost. Jesus Christ lives in you!

You are a Wolf Shocker! That wolf has just put the grab on an **Attack Lamb**!

JESUS, OUR EXAMPLE

When the Devil came against Jesus in the wilderness, who was in trouble? Was Jesus in trouble? Never. He is the King of kings and the Lord of lords. He is the same yesterday, today, and forever! He is not now, nor has He ever been less than the Devil. It was the Devil who was in trouble. He was being set up for defeat on the earth. And the good news is when he tries to sink those wolfly claws into you, he is being set up again!

Why would Jesus want you to walk around and entrap the Devil? Why would He lead you into places where the Enemy operates? Why would He call you and send you into places of demonic strength? Because it is His ultimate purpose that every man woman and child have the opportunity to receive Him. He knows where the obstacles dwell and He has included you in His purpose as an Attack Lamb to set to flight those enemies of the Gospel which have hindered people from hearing His name.

Why doesn't He just blast them Himself and have it done? This is my question every day. Because He has chosen to include the Church in His plan to reach the nations. I have debated with Him just as Moses did over Israel. I have expressed my frustration over people who will not pray, or give, or go. He always has the same response, "Pray ye the Lord of the harvest..."

You're an Attack Lamb in the army of Jesus Christ. But as you go forth in the guise of a sheep, you are directed by His voice, word, and sovereign providence. Like a spy with a constant communication's uplink to headquarters, you have the perfect cover. You're a sheep. Who would suspect anything from a sheep?

FINDING THE GAPS

There are gaps all around you. They have become the caverns of daily living from which the wolves prey upon those who have not yet met Christ. As an Attack Lamb it is your job to walk about and see where the wolves are. You are a spy for the Lord walking about the promised land of your school, your community, your place of work. You are there to discern and neutralize the powers that hold back your friends from receiving Jesus as their Lord.

Tomorrow morning as you prepare for work, ask the Lord to use you as an Attack Lamb. You will have a different sort of day. You will be walking as the housing for the Lion of the Tribe of Judah. Might as well wear a "Wolves Beware" shirt. You will go to that place of work or study and it will look totally different to you. You will see it in the perspective of an heavenly vision. As you enter, many angels will be there with you. The elders will be catching the prayers you offer and pouring them out before the throne. The beasts will be bowing down and crying, "Holy, holy, holy is the Lord."

Imagine the look on your colleague's face as the radiant power of Jesus flows forth from your eyes. You are going to perceive how the Enemy has worked in that place, and how you are going to neutralize him in the lives of those for whom Christ died. I am so glad you are there. In that gap. Waiting for the Lord to move through you. Pray, pray, pray.

YOUR PLACE IN THE SPACE

You have a place in the space between man and God. It's called **Intercession**, and it is the second letter in our **S-I-N-G** acrostic.

You are His ambassador to men, and their advocate with Him (2 Corinthians 5:20). What an important place to be. That is why you are who you are, live where you do, shop where you do, were hired where you work, and went to school where you did. The Lord has had His hand on you all the time. He has ordered your steps to accomplish His ultimate purpose. Now you are in that gap between He and them. What should you do?

Matthew 10 is an instruction manual for Attack Lambs. It addresses specific ministry, the power we have, the way to travel, the amount of money we need, how to know where we should stay, how to react when ill-treated. All of life is defined for us in those verses.

Verse 27 is our labor management agreement. **"What I tell you in darkness, that speak ye in light; and what you hear [whispered] in the ear, that preach ye upon the housetops."** We are going to see into the heavenly realm and then act in the earthly one. We are going to hear the direction of God and have the boldness to do it. This prayer stuff is all right! Have you ever heard a deal like that?

You go into the gaps in your town and wait on the Lord. He will show you the heavenly vision and the way to reach the people there. When you have that word, you can do as He has shown you and you will be a winner of souls!

A DAY IN PITTSBURGH, IN THE GAP

One day I was standing in a doorway in downtown Pittsburgh. There is a large bus stop and a welfare office on the corner. People deal drugs there and make contacts for different things. The police are there, but they are outnumbered. As long as everything flows along in a peaceful way, they remain calm.

That day I was standing there with the motor running; that is to say, I was praying softly in tongues. I was there and a young man separated himself from the crowd and walked over to me. I had no sign. I was not passing out tracts, although I love to do that. I was just standing there with the motor running and this young man walked right up to me as though he had been told to go see me. Then, without either of us saying "hello," he began to speak.

"I'm sorry," he said in a mournful drone. "I'm so sorry."

"Excuse me?" I responded gently.

"I'm sorry for my life," he continued. "My life is a mess."

"Tell Jesus your sorry," I said softly. "He can forgive you."

"Jesus, I'm sorry," his drone continued. "Forgive me, my life is a mess."

We stood there quietly for a few minutes. I heard nothing by the Spirit to say, so I said nothing. I saw nothing to do, so I did nothing. After a few moments he turned to me and held out his hand.

"Thank you so much," he said with joy. "Thank you so much." His face shown and he squared up his shoulders, and with a smile on his face walked happily up the street.

The peace and presence of God touched his lost soul. I saw the transformation in his eyes and heard it in his voice. It was one of the most beautiful miracles I've ever witnessed. That young man had found forgiveness.

No sign, no PA system, no tracts, just being in that gap with the motor running. **The end result of successful spiritual warfare is souls saved.** This is the reason Jesus has invested His great power in us. This is the reason you are reading this book. Think about all that had to happen for you to read this sentence. Jesus had to put together a wonderful plan to equip you as an Attack Lamb and He did it. Wow, you are a part of a great plan. You are a worker in His harvest. You are so special.

THE NO NAME WARRIORS

In the tenth chapter of the gospel of Luke, we see seventy others going forth. I love these guys. They were the No-Names of the New Testament. Attack Lambs, every one. They came to the Lord in response to the prayer for workers and they were ready to be sent. Jesus gives them the same power He gave the apostles. They can cast out devils, heal the sick, raise the dead, give eyesight to the blind. Man, these are some kind of sheep among wolves.

They have a great time of ministry and return to give Him their report. They tell Jesus what, to them, is the most exciting thing, **"...even the devils are subject unto us through thy Name"** (Luke 10:17). Jesus understood their excitement, I'm sure. But He called them back to a greater cause for rejoicing, namely that their names were written down in heaven.

He was requiring proper perspective from them. Why? Because all power flows from relationship with the source of that power. In this case, from the Lord Himself. Maintain that relationship and we won't have to worry about power.

There is truly no greater cause for celebration than our salvation. Having said that, the disciple's report is still true. Demons **are** subject to the name of Jesus.

These seventy disciples used a wonderful word in their report. They said the devils are subject unto us. This word *subject* is the Greek word which we transliterate, *hupotasso*. It means to "voluntarily order yourself under the affairs of another." We most often translate this word as "submit."

When you join a church, you *"hupotasso."* You submit. You see what time the services begin and you arrange your schedule to be on time. You do this through several acts of your will. You determine to be there. You set other schedule entries around that fixed time.

When you marry, you *"hupotasso."* You submit. You spend years listening to your intended's plans and you order your steps to accommodate that plan. You submit to each other in the fear of God. You prefer one another and live to see the other's dreams fulfilled. You do this voluntarily. It is an act of your will. You determine to leave all other plans and people and to cleave to your spouse and to be one in Christ.

Successful marriages reflect this principle of *hupotasso.* A marriage breaks apart as soon as one party determines to have their will, their way, upon their demands. Love does not demand, it seeks to serve.

You also apply the principle of *huppotasso* where you work. You have a set time to be there to keep the business running well for the benefit of all. You set the events of your life voluntarily so that the best production possible is accomplished. You have seen that the Lord honors those who submit. *Huppotasso* is a big word with Him.

The seventy others reported to the Lord that as they went about in the gaps of their world, the devils voluntarily submitted to them. This was not a dialogue with demons. This was not shouting at a lying spirit to give his name. (I have always wondered how a lying spirit was going to do that.) This was not pouring oil down a person's throat to have them vomit up a spirit of this or that. This is power through prayer. This is authority on the scene. The devils **voluntarily** ordered themselves under this authority.

THE ODD ANSWER

Jesus gave his seventy disciples what I have always considered an odd answer when they returned rejoicing over the demons being subject to them. He declared, **"I saw Satan fall like lightning from heaven "** (Luke 10:17 NKJV). What He was saying was, the battle has already been won. Satan and his demonic band have already lost and forfeited their place in heaven. His power, and therefore his authority, has been broken. Naturally the demons who operate under Satan's broken authority would be subject to the name of Jesus in the lives of the people to whom they went. Through this same fact of our authority in the name of Jesus the devils are subject to us today. The Enemy is cast down still today by the name of Jesus.

So now, the question of our century. Why has the world not been reached with the good news of Jesus?

Answer: because we do not go to them. Why do we not go to them and declare this glorious Gospel of good news that Jesus has set them free?

Two reasons. First, we are too busy with our own stuff, too self-involved, self-oriented and selfish. Second, we think we **are** sheep. But we are not!

BE WHAT YOU ARE

Jesus has made you an Attack Lamb. The devils will order themselves under you; the power of the Devil is broken in your life. Get out there and bash some wolves! Use what God has given you. Jesus said to these no-name warriors, **"I give you the authority...over all the power of the enemy, *and nothing shall by any means hurt you"*** (Luke 10:19 NKJV emphasis added).

Attack Lambs do not sit back and let the pusher take their kids! They get out there in the gap and pray! Attack Lambs do not allow the Devil to kill an entire generation of babies! They get out there and pray. You will find

Attack Lambs in doorways, standing quietly on street corners, walking around government buildings, in the audience of the Senate and Parliament. You will find them in tour groups of the White House and in the Forbidden City of China. You will find them in business in Riyadh and booking flights to Mecca. You will find Attack Lambs in every sector of society.

They are spying out the land. They are driving out the devils. They are neutralizing the effect of Satan on the world's population, and all the while they look like gentle little lambs at play. I tell you the truth, in all the places I have walked, I have not raised my voice above a conversational tone. I have caused no demonstration but, in the power of the Holy Spirit through prayer, I have seen walls come down, gremlins leave Kremlins, abortion clinics close and young men walk up to repent.

You are an Attack Lamb. You have power over all the devices of the Devil. Get out there. Set apart one lunch per week and fast and walk around the place where you work and pray for the people. Pray for workers, pray for open doors, pray for fruit for every Christian ministry and business, pray for a financial/material flow to prosper the Gospel in that place.

You are an Attack Lamb. Take one morning a week and get out to that local school. Walk around that place or get to a convenient place to pray and wait upon the Lord. Pray for workers, doors, fruit, and finances. Look and listen to the heavenly vision for that place. Cry out to God for the people. Walk around and make those devils voluntarily bow down. They will for it is the word of God and it is true. It is not by might or power that these children shall be loosed, it is by the Spirit of the Lord as you get into that gap between God and man and cry out for those souls. Get on out there. It is for His purpose that you were born. Fulfill your destiny, get in that gap.

THE SECRET

We were starting a Christian School in a small Pennsylvania community. There was resistance from the school board to allow us the rented use of an existing school building. They just would not even put the topic on their agenda.

Meeting after meeting, we went and just sat there. We looked very foolish to them. Our prayers were constant and we waited on the Lord to see how He was going to accomplish His desire to train up young men and women in His ways. The members of the board did not recognize us or give us any opportunity to speak. They were trying to pretend we were not even there.

In actual fact, it was not these men and women with whom we were doing battle. It was a combined spiritual force which we shall detail when we get to the "N" in our acrostic. We were sitting there as Attack Lambs.

For several months we sent letters asking to be heard, then we would sit and pray and have no response. We were encouraged to cause a demonstration, but thought it not Lamb like. We claimed *huppotasso* power and rejoiced in our salvation. I must say the school board meetings in that town were quite boring.

Finally one night as the board was leaving one of the members passing me stopped. He turned and said, "Aren't you Mark Geppert?"

I assured him I was.

"Didn't I used to fix your father's car?" he asked.

I assured him he had.

"Are you part of this group?" He looked at the three of us.

I said I was, and asked if he had seen our letters.

"Come next month," he said.

That was it for direction.

VICTORY IN JESUS

We used that building for years and finally bought it. The Lord delivered it into our hands through a mechanic who sat with doctors, deciding issues in a school from which he had never graduated. Attack Lambs learn to rejoice in Jesus and wait for Him to move for them.

Attack Lambs are spies for Jesus. We are His eyes in the earth. As we maintain a heavenly vision, He leads us to the caverns of wolves. He causes us to stand at the mouth of their dens and pray. As we do, sometimes the wolves attempt to attack us. You are irresistible to them. However, when the name of Jesus is invoked, they voluntarily order themselves under you. Since you are voluntarily ordered under Jesus, the power of the Enemy in that place is neutralized and the Gospel can go forth. As you walk in His presence, you will manifest His power and accomplish His purpose.

Jesus cautioned the seventy no-name disciples to keep the source of their joy rooted in the reality of their relationship with Him. He said not to rejoice over earthly success, but rather that we have relationship with the Father. This simple statement is the SECRET to victory in spiritual warfare. Remember, all power flows out of relationship to the source of that power.

As we go into the gap, looking for all the world like little sheep, the power of God goes with us. We are the temple of the Holy Ghost. We are a home for the Lion of the tribe of Judah. He will manifest His great power when the wool is pulled from us.

The **S**, which stands for **"Spy** out the land," in our acrostic is very thrilling, but wait until you find out about the "**I**."

CHAPTER 7
Park The Ark

G od told Moses, "Build a box.
"Use simple acacia wood.
"Cover it with gold on the outside.
"Cover it with gold on the inside.
"Put three things in the box.
  "The tablets of the Law,
  "A pot of manna,
  "And Aaron's rod that budded.
"Put a gold covered lid on the box.
"Put a crown of gold around the lid.
"Stand an angel with wings extended over the box on one side.
"Stand an angel with wings extended over the box on the other side.
"Within the crown and under their wings is the mercy seat.
"Sprinkle the blood of the lamb of sacrifice on the mercy seat.
"My Presence will dwell in power above the mercy seat.

And flow out to the people from there" (Exodus 25, author's paraphrase)

The "box" would be called the ark of the testimony. It was made of simple wood and covered with gold. Three things were placed in it: the tablets of the Law, carved by God Himself, a pot of the perfect food which sustained the nation of Israel for forty years—manna, and Aaron's rod that budded to validate his divine call to leadership. A lid was placed on the box and a crown was placed around the lid. Inserted into the crown was a piece of wood covered in gold called the "mercy seat." Blood was sprinkled on that mercy seat.

On either side of the mercy seat angels were placed, facing each other with their wings extended. The glory of God came and dwelt between the angels above the mercy seat. The presence of God was there in power.

THE PHILISTINE'S MISTAKE

Like the Devil in the wilderness and the wolves in our world, the Philistines made a big mistake. They captured the ark (1 Samuel 5). And to make matters worse they put it in the temple of the false god of the Philistines, Dagon. They closed the temple up to secure their treasure and spent the night in celebration.

The Philistines imagined the ark itself to be the god of the Israelites, and that it was an idol like theirs. They attributed the power of Israel to the box, knowing nothing of the power presence of God dwelling there.

In the morning they opened the door of the temple and the god Dagon had fallen forward and was face down in front of the ark of the covenant. It had bowed down to the ark. Actually the Power Presence of God had fulfilled the coming Word that **"every knee shall bow and every tongue confess that Jesus Christ is Lord to the glory of the Father"** (Philippians 2:10-11 paraphrased).

Puzzled but determined, the Philistines propped

their god back up and closed the door again. The next morning an even greater surprise awaited them. This time, not only had Dagon again bowed down before the ark, but now his head, hands and feet were broken off. The head is a symbol of plans and strategies, the hands of power and authority, and the feet of the ability to stand. Dagon had no ability to devise a plan that would stand before the ark, nor any power or authority in the presence of the God of Israel.

CONNECTING THE DOTS

Now I want you to pay close attention here. We are going to connect some dots for you so you can see the whole picture. Did the ark shout? No. Did it jump up and down and sound crazy? No. All it did was sit there, parked. It was the presence of the glory of the Lord that did the work. The false god bowed down. It had to. The victory was in the power of the presence of God.

And here is the connection, saint... **Your victories are through the same power. You are the modern day ark.** Yes, you are!

Let's connect some more dots. Jesus took you, simple material. He formed you to contain a testimony. He covered you on the outside and the inside with the precious gold of His righteousness. You look good to those around you and your character is being refined through the power of the Holy Spirit.

Like the tablets of the Law in the ark, He has placed His Word in your heart that you might not sin against Him.

Like the manna in the ark reminded the Israelites of God's provision, you too have the provision of God not only for your daily bread but for the bread of life itself in Jesus.

Just as Aaron's budding rod reminded the Jews of God's power to bring life to that which was dead, God has given you the power to speak life to those who are dead in their own sins and trespasses. You have the authority in the name of Jesus to break the bondages that cripple the people whom God loves. You have the power of the rod that budded.

As a believer in Jesus you, like no people ever on the face of the earth, have the Holy Spirit of God Himself dwelling in you. **You**, saint, are God's ark of the covenant today!

He closed the box. That is, He has sealed the testimony within you by the Holy Spirit. He has rimmed the box with a crown calling you a royal priesthood, a holy nation that you should show forth His praises.

Just like the blood of the sacrifice was placed on the mercy seat of the ark, the Father has covered you with the blood of His own dear Son. When He looks on you, He sees the blood in which there is no flaw. He knows your every weakness and still calls you righteous. How great is that blood! He has placed angels on either side of you. Yes, it's true, you are a protected property, the object of His limitless love. Every demon who attempts to bring you down has to get through those two angels! Double coverage is wonderful.

He has come to dwell between those angels, above the mercy seat in your heart. Because of the blood of Jesus, God can now dwell with you and in you. His glory flows out thorough your eyes in His compassion for a lost world, through your hands in healing, through your mouth as you speak the words of eternal life, and through your feet as you walk the land and pray.

Just as the presence of God went with the ark releasing tremendous power, so too does His presence within you. Wherever the presence of the Lord is there is liberty. As you move about your place of work or school or home, you bring release.

THE PROTOTYPE

What the Philistines really had when they had the ark was the Attack Lamb prototype. As an Attack Lamb you can enter the gaps of your world. You can sense the presence of the wolves. You park your ark in that presence and allow the glory to flow. The forces at work there to resist the Gospel must *hupotasso* (submit) because of Him who dwells in you.

Go ahead, think of a place of tension. Perhaps you are trying to clean out your child's room. Those posters and CD's are a symbol to you of the power that is trying to capture the soul of your young one. Stand in there and gently praise the Lord. Allow the Holy Spirit in you to rise and live big. Perhaps the Lord will give you an instruction to do something. Obey it.

Did you practice His presence in that room? Imagine what you can do with this Power Presence. You could walk around your town. You could walk about the schools. You could go to centers of racial strife or public corruption and, through the Power Presence of God, you could be used of God to change your city!

You are the ark. God wants to lead you into the presence of the false gods which hold society in their demonic grip. Keep your focus on Jesus and park that ark, and you will begin to see both small and dramatic changes.

It is the will of God that every man woman and child have the opportunity to receive Jesus Christ as their personal Lord and Savior in this generation. This spiritual work must be done in a spiritual way. These people are held captive by the Dagons of today, and you are the ark which the Lord wants to position in the gaps to cause that false god to bow down. You will not have to shout, jump or scream. In fact, you will appear as an irrelevant or extraneous circumstance in that gap. Go for it!

In the next chapter we will look at the Dagons of today, and how they can be brought down.

CHAPTER 8
Know Your Enemy

Pinch yourself. That's right, gently pinch yourself. Are you flesh and blood? I thought so. If you are not flesh and blood, please put this book down and slowly walk away.

Now look at the person nearest you. It could be your wife, husband, or friend. Maybe they are a close colleague or client. If you can do so without starting a riot, pinch them. Flesh and blood, right? If they are not flesh and blood, close this book and get off the bus, leave the room, or simply keep your seat and pray.

We do not wrestle against flesh and blood. Please stop wrestling with yourself. Be freed from asking if you are good enough, mature enough, tall enough, thin enough or trained enough to be used by the Lord in prayer. Anyone can pray! This is not about the ark, it is about the power. God is at work.

Look at the person you just pinched. Please do not wrestle with other people. So much time is wasted as we try to get the upper hand in relationships. Life is too short for power plays in the church and at work. We are on the earth to win these people, not to offend them. It is the will of God that they have the opportunity to receive Jesus and you are there to pray for them. Stop wrestling with people.

So many in the church today are carrying the disappointment of broken relationships. Divorce has cut deeply into the lives of two generations. Broken promises and dashed dreams have filled cities with heartsick despair. Businesses fail, contracts are broken, violence erupts all because of broken relationships. But, good news, there is a way to defeat the devices of the Enemy and free yourself and loved ones from such darkness.

THE KEY TO VICTORY

In 2 Corinthians 2:10 we read we must forgive in the name of Jesus. We must stop wrestling with people who have disappointed us. Can you imagine a lamb wrestling with a person? Or worse, how about two lambs wrestling with each other. If you want to be victorious in wrestling the Enemy's forces then you must first forgive those who are flesh and blood. Let's do it now.

Just pray with me saying, **"In the name of Jesus I forgive every person living or dead who ever hurt me, used me, or abused me in any way. I release them into the hands of the Lord that they might know Him as their personal Lord and Savior. Father, I ask you to save them in Jesus name."**

As we were praying you might have thought of someone in particular. Go ahead, I'll wait while you forgive them by name. Use the name of Jesus. "Father, in the name of Jesus I forgive_____, and ask you to bless them with the knowledge of your Son. I release them to your blessing."

I call this "Rolodex™ prayer." I pray this prayer every so often to make sure I'm not keeping score on anybody. If you never create an enemy or take an offense then you do not have to go through this kind of prayer; but, life is relational and we can be offended, so we must be quick to pray.

The Devil loves to create strife because, as long as your time is taken up wrestling with people, you will not be free to take on the forces which hold the world's population in bondage to darkness. To be effective in spiritual warfare, you must walk free from offense.

Good, now that we have established we are **not** wrestling flesh and blood, let's give our attention to the forces with which we **do** wrestle. Paul researched this as he moved about from culture to culture and nation to nation, and has given us a very clear list of the Dagons of today.

THE FACES OF THE ENEMY

Our King James Bible calls the spiritual forces Paul's identified as:

> Principalities
> Powers
> Rulers of the darkness of this world
> Spiritual wickedness in high places

But to better understand them let's take a look at the actual words Paul used in the Greek[1].

ARCHAS

The first is the **archas**[2]. This word is transliterated Greek for the word which appears in the Ephesians 6:12 text as "principalities." It is used many times throughout the Bible. It is often translated "beginning." It carries the sense of preeminence, the "We were here first" attitude that becomes territorial. The *archas* operates through **intimidation.**

Have you wrestled with this lately? How about the

home where we modify all behavior to prevent an explosion of emotion from one of the family members? Do you know any people who try to dominate their families through this force?

What about the employer or manager who can not receive feedback from their colleagues without going into a rage? Or the teacher or coach who controls through fear. These are operating in the *archas*. It is **not** the flesh and blood, it **is** the power working behind them.

Your strategy, as God's instrument, is to park your ark in the gap between these folks and the Lord...and pray. As you have discerned the presence of the *archas*, you can now neutralize the impact by focusing on Jesus instead of the problem, and praying for the people.

Practice the Power Presence in that gap. If not for yourself, for the others who are under the influence of this force. Get in that place, Attack Lamb, and watch the Lord cause Dagon to bow down.

Recently I was teaching this point in a Prayer Walking Seminar in one of the great churches of Asia. Fifteen hundred had gathered and, as we shared about this point, there came the gripping realization that we had hit on a truth relevant to this people. We had touched a spiritual nerve. They shifted in their seats, nodded, smiled and I could see that their hearts were being touched.

The Asians are a very humble people with a low self-esteem. Actually, I think they have a great self esteem, but by the inflated standard of the West, they appear to be insecure or intimidated. Certainly, the Asians of that city have conformed to a very legalistic society where you adapt or die.

At the conclusion of the meeting, the pastor rose to lead the people in a declaration against the *archas* to remove the intimidation from their midst. As that false god bowed down, the people began to applaud. For many minutes we were caught up in the joy of release as the Power Presence brought liberty to God's people. They were no longer bound.

In the subsequent six months they added a thousand new members to the church It is the will of God that the *archas* be broken so that men and women, boys and girls, can receive Jesus Christ as their personal Lord and Savior.

But the Devil's bag of tricks doesn't stop with just one evil force. The next one we will consider is formidable as well.

EXOUSIAS

The second force listed as "powers" is the **exousias**[3], again a transliteration from the Greek word. This word is often translated "authority." When the scribes heard the teaching of Jesus they proclaimed, "From whence comes this teaching, He teaches with **authority.**"

The root thought of the word is "**the right to speak.**" Think about that for a minute. Is there any greater debate in society than who has the right to speak, to express themselves? This is the root force which has suppressed minorities and women throughout history. How many children have been aborted because they do not yet make a sound outside the womb?

This is the issue which makes salesmen, bankers, and attorneys the favored candidates for church leadership. They are appointed and elected because they can present themselves well. Sadly, many wonderful Christian people have eliminated themselves from Christian service because they do not speak well. Moses did. When God called him to be His agent of deliverance for Israel he attempted to defer saying he couldn't do the job because he did not speak well. Tradition says possibly he stuttered.

He certainly could write though. He sure could pray. He was very good at miracles. But, because of the *exousias* stronghold, he declined the call until persuaded by the Lord.

Prayer, on the other hand, is wonderful because everyone can do it. I tell you God hears the simplest prayer and, if prayed according to His will, He grants the petition. If you are praying that every man, woman, and child have the opportunity to receive Christ, you are praying according to the will of God. Keep on praying that way and you will see people come to Christ all around you because you are speaking to the Lord.

No power above, on, or under the earth can keep you from speaking to your heavenly Father. The way has been opened for you though the blood of Jesus Christ; you have access to the throne. You are called to see heaven's vision for man. Get in that gap and talk to your Father about the souls of those around you and do not ever again wonder if you have the right to do so. The power of *exousias* is broken.

In fact, the issue has been settled forever. Look at Zechariah 3:2. There you will find where God got fed up with Satan and told him to shut up. Do you see it there? Satan was standing before the throne of God and Jesus was there, and when the Devil stepped up to speak and resist Him, the Lord said to Satan, **"The Lord rebuke thee, O Satan:....."**

The Devil can no longer deny anyone who is in Christ the right to speak. There is neither Jew nor Greek, neither black nor white. Neither Asian nor Caucasian. There is no difference between man or woman. We are one in Christ and we all have the right to pray. We have the right to see the heavenly vision and to communicate it here in the earth. It is the will of God and the gates of hell will not be able to withstand the army of Attack Lambs going forth to park the ark and practice the presence of the power of God.

Don't you dare say you cannot speak, or that you don't have anything to say. You can pray and that is what is important. If we ask anything according to His will He hears us and grants the petition we desire of Him. Get out there in that gap and claim those souls and you will have the happiest day of your life!

Forgive me for getting carried away with this one, but I have seen so many wonderful Christian people exclude themselves from ministry unnecessarily because of the fear of speaking. I used to get horrible upset stomachs and nose bleeds before I had to speak. My thoughts would ramble all over the place. I would sweat and get hives. Then I realized I was wrestling with a spiritual force. It wasn't the people, they loved me. They were listening.

Once I stood against that *exousias*, I found victory. I found I was not bound by the fear of man. I found I did have the right and ability to proclaim Christ in the power of the Holy Spirit. You do too. Come on, it starts with prayer.

KOSMOKRATOS

The third force is the **kosmokratos**[4], in English, "rulers of the darkness of this world."

The people who operate under the influence of this force are easy to see, they **use people to get things**. The American church has been inundated with the *kosmokratos*. About every three years I am approached by people who want me to refer them to church leaders and members so they can sell them everything from soap to mutual funds. The pitch is always the same, "We will give a percentage of our profits to missions."

I do not mean to be unkind, but to use the church as a development bed for multi-level marketing schemes is as far from the Great Commission as anyone can get. The inference that a percentage will be given to reach people who are on their way to hell's fires and eternal damnation is offensive. The truth is unless you are giving all that you are, all that you have, and all that you hope to be to the will of God, you are falling short of the glory God intends for you.

My solution is...write the check now. Give what you have now and apply your time to prayer and the will of God. Most recently I was approached to offer "networking" business opportunities to wealthy Asians whom I have met. Wealthy Asians are those who were able to preserve money and family through the Japanese occupation of their country. They honor their ancestors in a way that few Westerners will ever understand. They did not become wealthy rapidly and they do not believe in fast friendships. My relationship with them has nothing to do with their money. To use those relationships for financial gain, even with the promise of a percentage coming to the ministry, is a form of prostitution to their way of thinking.

I enter their cities to pray. I see where the *kosmocratos* forces are operating. I walk and intercede for the people there and they are saved. My relationship to them in is the spirit, not in the *kosmos*. This blending of motive in the church is indicative of the *kosmokratos* spirit at work in our midst.

Where is the *kosmokratos* operating in your town? Some areas which come to my mind are prostitution, pornography, abortion clinics, and drug traffic. These are areas of great commerce. We do not often look at them as spiritual force manifestation, but that is what they are.

Attack Lambs, get out there and drive off those wolves. Get the ark out there and practice the Power Presence and drive out this force of corruption. Free the people in spirit so they will hear the Gospel when you or another presents it. You could be the one who stands on the corner and prays, and gets to see a tract passer find success. Imagine looking through the cloud of the presence of God and seeing a group of youths give their lives to Christ because you have broken the peer group bondage brought on through marketing devices.

You can pray. You can park the ark with the motor running and reach heaven on behalf of those young people. They do not have to be the target of every marketing scheme. They do not have to wear certain clothes, use drugs, listen to crazy music and talk in an undiscernable dialect. You can set them free through prayer. God wants to work through you to reach them.

PNEUMA TAE PONERIAS

The fourth force Paul mentions, "spiritual wickedness in high places, is the **pneuma tae ponerias**[5].

These is the **spirit of malice**. Webster says that malice is the premeditated harm of, or the desire to injure, another human being. This is the force which directs mass murder. In America, we kill approximately 4,000 unborn children every day. This is the biggest mass murder in the history of the human race. Our nation will decline as long as we remain unrepentant for this action. Through the *pneuma tae ponerias*, our nation and the rest of the world is being driven into spiritual, financial, and ecological disaster.

America is not alone in its bent to self-destruction. There are mobs in Korea, Skinheads in Europe, nerve gas cults in Japan, and the military in China. "Ethnic cleansing" has become the accepted term for the spirit of malice in many nations. As men brutalize their countrymen around the world, we are to believe this is little more than an expression of territorial ethnicity.

Believe that if you will, but the apostle Paul says we are wrestling with a spirit of malice. We, the Attack Lambs, the gap fillers, must take our Power Presence arks into the gaps and strategic locations of the earth's populations and, under the impact of the heavenly vision, must stand against this force.

Once, in Irkutsk, Siberia, we saw a little plant that had pushed its way up through asphalt paving to greet the Spring sun and we knew that no matter how thick the darkness, the Lord would revive Russia.

We stood against the poverty and prayed especially for our brothers and sisters in Siberia who lived in abject poverty. So many hours we had lamented over them as we traveled the Trans-Siberian region as mobile arks for Jesus.

From 1985 through 1988 we prayed, traveled, networked, and prayed again. In '88 there was a breakthrough as an attempted coup failed, and the Director of Ideology was replaced by a man favorable to the church. A greater freedom came to the church; the Dagon bowed.

Shortly, we will discover the pressure points that change a nation, the five specific places you should go to pray and bring God's Power Presence to bear. But, first we must talk about the Name that is above every name.

CHAPTER 9
Name Above All Names

The fragrant fumes of burning joss sticks filled the temple with a mystical haze. The Tien Fu Gong Temple is a worship center for thousands. From my position to the left of the rear altar, I could see the tourist buses unloading their curious crowds.

The fortune tellers called out. Spiritual hucksters. They displayed their diagrams and tools before them and offered to plunge into the depths of the spirit realm to tell these Europeans something of their future.

Inside the temple the medium was asleep, the result I think of the combination of the smoke and our little group of intercessors. He always takes a nap from noon till closing we found out. A very scary fellow with long lashes and a totally stoned expression on his gaunt little face. He often reminded me of a hobbit perched on his stool.

A tourist couple in their thirties approached me, "Excuse me," the lady said, "do you work here?"

I was indeed working there. My ark had been parked for several hours at that point. "Yes, I am working here." I responded, wondering how the Lord was going to reach these two.

"Could you tell me where I could find a kitchen god?" she asked with such earnest I was startled. Looking at their size you could see her cooking was neither bad nor lacking.

"That would be at the altar surface level," I answered, "among the domestics."

I motioned toward the altar which had three levels: the *heavenlies*, the *earthiest*, (or surface level) and the *nether world*. They are the representation of the structure of the ancestral worship system which has evolved in all of Asia.

"You may not take the idols," I told her, "but you might want to talk to the medium if he wakes up." I hoped his appearance would dispel her interest.

At that point her husband entered the conversation. "What do you do here?" he asked. "I am a Christian missionary," I began to explain.

He was startled and a bit confused. "Well, what are you doing here then?"

Well, since you asked, I thought. Here was my God-provided opportunity.

"I am here praying for the Chinese that they will be set free from the power of these forces. I am declaring to them that Jesus has defeated the Devil in the heavens, on the earth, and under the earth, and that He has a name that is above all names. That at the name of Jesus every knee shall bow."

My answer was made more effective by the smoke and stench of idolatry which filled our lungs and eyes, causing them to water.

Their curiosity was aroused. They had never heard anything like that. We stepped into an open courtyard and continued our conversation. They assured me they were Christians, traveling on an Asian tour package. This temple was part of their itinerary and they were fascinated by the diversity of culture. They didn't really want a kitchen god, they just wanted to see one, and had not realized how deeply their host nation was bound by spiritual forces.

With a reaffirmation of their faith in Jesus, they boarded the bus and continued the tour. I returned to the gap which the Lord had assigned for the day. I placed myself beside the altar and once again began interceding for the people as they came to offer sacrifices to the idols. How my heart ached for each one that they might know the joy of life with Jesus.

The Dagons of today are operating in many temples. You and I, as the modern day ark of God's covenant in Jesus, must go to those places and establish the lordship of Jesus, invoking His name and speaking what the Holy Spirit gives us to say.

THE DEFEATED FOE

Ezekiel 28:11-20 tells us the Devil was an "anointed cherub" whose job was to convey praise and worship to God in the heavenly service. But iniquity was found in him. He attempted to ascend to the throne of God and was cast down.

He will be placed in fire which will come forth from him and will be utterly destroyed before those through whom he used to traffic.

Isaiah 14 makes the point that Satan was cast down from the heavens. Remember, Jesus told the disciples He had seen Satan fall like lightening. **Jesus has defeated the Devil in the heavenlies.**

Then, in Matthew 4, Jesus went into the wilderness after He was baptized and defeated the Devil on the earth. What great news this is! How we rejoiced when the Lion of the tribe of Judah commanded the Enemy to "get thee hence." **Jesus has defeated the Devil on the earth.**

Finally, in Ephesians 4 Jesus descended into hell and for three days sought out the Devil. Having found him,

Jesus put his foot on his head and took the keys of death and hell away from him. Then, with the battle won, the Holy Spirit caused Christ to rise, and passing through Abraham's bosom, He led those captive there to freedom. **So Jesus has defeated the Devil under the earth.**

You see Jesus, as the Attack Lamb Prototype, defeated the Enemy in all three areas of temptation. The victory of Jesus Christ is complete in the heavenlies, in the earth, and under the earth!

The third part of our acrostic **S-I-N-G** is the <u>name</u> of Jesus, the <u>Name</u> above all names.

Paul describes the Lion of Judah emerging from the Lamb of God.

> **Wherefore God also hath highly exalted him, and given him a name which is above every name: that at the name of Jesus every knee should bow, of *things in heaven, and things in earth, and things under the earth;* and that every tongue should confess that Jesus Christ is Lord, to the glory of God the Father.**
> **Philippians 2:9-11** (emphasis added)

HIS GLORY...OUR GLORY

The glory of God which dwells between the angels above the mercy seat in our lives, dwells there because of the name of Jesus. Had Christ not come, the blood would not have been applied and His powerful Presence would not have been able to abide with men. Through His death on the cross, Jesus made it possible for the will of the Father to be accomplished and God's desired fellowship with man was restored. He does not want any to perish. Therefore, He has commanded a spiritual people to bear His Presence in the earth in such a way that it will cause the Dagons to bow down and the souls of men to be released.

Romans 8:5-11 clearly states that to be effective in

the purpose of God we must be spiritually minded. This is possible only when the Spirit of Christ dwells in us. Those who are "in the flesh," that is, having their thinking oppressed by the influence of the *archas, exousias, kosmokratos,* and *ponerias,* cannot please God.

The focus of an Attack Lamb must be Jesus, the Lamb sacrificed for us. It is from Him we receive the patience, love, mercy, and compassion to endure the assaults and contradictions of the four forces of the Enemy mentioned before.

Paul goes further to say that you are not in the flesh if the Spirit of Christ is in you (Romans 8). Bold statement that it is, it stands nevertheless.

When we name the name of Jesus and accept Him as our salvation, the *archas, exousias, kosmokratos,* and *ponerias* must bow down in our lives. The more we forgive in Jesus' name, the more free we become to love others and to reach them with the good news of the Gospel. The name of Jesus will set us free to set others free. This is the Christian experience. There is power in His name!

PULLING DOWN YOUR STRONGHOLDS

Second Corinthians 10:1-6 gives a description of the "strongholds" in our lives. The only use of the term in the New Testament, this verse is a key in understanding the Power Presence of God, and His flow through us.

Now I Paul myself beseech you by the meekness and gentleness of Christ, who in presence am base among you, but being absent am bold toward you: but I beseech you, that I may not be bold when I am present with that confidence, wherewith I think to be bold against some, which think of us as if we walked according to the flesh. For though we walk in the flesh, we do not war after the flesh: (For the weapons of our

warfare are not carnal, but mighty through God to the pulling down of strong holds;) casting down imaginations, and every high thing that exalteth itself against the knowledge of God, and bringing into captivity every thought to the obedience of Christ; and having in a readiness to revenge all disobedience when your obedience is fulfilled.

2 Corinthians 10:1-6

The warfare in which we are engaged as Attack Lambs is the neutralization of the tactics of the *archas, exousias, kosmokratos*, and *ponerias* as we see them lift themselves up in our minds and in the culture in which we live. How do we do this? By bringing the thoughts stimulated by these four forces into subjection to the knowledge of Jesus Christ.

Let's say that tomorrow you go to work, and there is competition between two divisions to see who is going to get an award. This is a carnal way of stimulating production. The incentive is a three-day trip to a beautiful island where you can just lay around in the sun and feel good about your employer.

Both divisions are asking employees to donate time to productivity so that the prize can be won. You know you are going to be pressured to do your share for your division. How do you bring this *kosmokratos-archas* force in subjection to the knowledge of Christ?

You set apart time in the morning and you pray. You ask the Lord to give you the courage and grace to serve your company as a good witness, but to be free from the manipulations. You then invoke the name of Jesus against those strongholds of imagination and manipulation. You remain in prayer until you feel a release in your spirit that the warfare is accomplished and you go off to work. You do your regular excellent job and ask the Lord to give you greater productivity throughout your normal day.

This sounds so simple, yet time after time I have seen it work. **Prayer which combines God's ultimate**

purpose with the invocation of the name of Jesus is incredibly powerful. Your being at that place of work is God's design to neutralize the four forces as they try to operate. Why? So that those around you will be able to receive Jesus Christ as their personal Lord and Savior.

Already, before even going to work, you are able to praise the Lord for the outcome. You have a witness in your spirit He has heard your prayer and, leaving the arm-twisting to Him, you begin to give Him praise. Remember, all successful spiritual endeavor comes forth from an attitude of praise and worship. The name of Jesus has been invoked, the Dagons will bow.

How do we know what the Lord wants to do in that office? Romans taught us we are led of the Spirit to fulfill the purpose of God. First Corinthians 2:9-16 goes on to tell us how. Let's look together at this very exciting passage.

> **But as it is written, Eye hath not seen, nor ear heard, neither have entered into the heart of man, the things which God hath prepared for them that love him. But God hath revealed them unto us by his Spirit: for the Spirit searcheth all things, yea, the deep things of God. For what man knoweth the things of a man, save the spirit of man which is in him? even so the things of God knoweth no man, but the Spirit of God. Now we have received not the spirit of the world, but the Spirit which is of God; that we might know the things that are freely given to us of God. Which things also we speak, not in the words which man's wisdom teacheth, but which the Holy Ghost teacheth; comparing spiritual things with spiritual. But the natural man receiveth not the things of the Spirit of God: for they are foolishness unto him: neither can he know them, because they are spiritually discerned. But he that is spiritual judgeth all things, yet he himself is judged of no man. For who**

hath known the mind of the Lord, that he may instruct him? But we have the mind of Christ.
1 Corinthians 2:9-16

Wow, that is a lot to read and understand, and yet it is very simple. You are an Attack Lamb. On the outside you are the most natural of all people. You are free from the four forces, you do not look like the world, but you do move about in it. As an Attack Lamb, you are led by the Lord's purpose. You approach your profession differently than those around you. You realize you are where you are so the Lord can reach others in the environment. You stay tuned in to the purpose of God in your life.

You know what the Lord is doing in that place because you are there in the name of Jesus. The others around you identify you as a Christian. You become a standard of right and wrong, and they are quick to let you know if you have transgressed their expectations. You set the standard for the place.

As the ark in the presence of Dagon, you are not invited to participate in many of the things which go on there. You are left to yourself and are able to gain tremendous leverage through kind words and prayer. When people have very real problems, they come by and drop them in your lap. You are God's point of contact for the people. He has brought you there to display relationship with the Father for them; to be the salt which makes them thirsty for Him.

You bring the things you see and hear into subjection to the word of God. In so doing you become a filter through which the devices of the *archas, exousias, kosmokratos*, and *ponerias* cannot pass. You are in the gap. In fact, when some approach your place of work, the worldly spirits in them will see the Lion in you and flee.

As you see those forces assault one of the flock God has given you there, you pray and they flee. That is why you are there. You are an intercessor. When you see the people as God sees them you will learn to love them as He does.

In Matthew's gospel Jesus defines His disciple's role, and ours, in that place of His Power Presence.

And I will give unto thee the keys of the kingdom of heaven: and whatsoever thou shalt bind on earth be bound in heaven: and whatsoever thou shalt loose on earth shalt be loosed in heaven. Then charged he his disciples that they should tell no man that he was Jesus the Christ.

Matthew 16:19

Why was the name of Jesus to be concealed at that time? Because He was still to go into the depths of hell and take the keys away from Satan. He still had to pay the price for our salvation. He was instructing the disciples in the power that would be theirs, and ours, **after** His resurrection from the dead.

Now, Jesus is risen from the dead. It's OK to shout as you read that. Now, Jesus is risen from the dead! He has defeated the Devil above, on, and under the earth. The keys work!

Remember in Zechariah 3 how the Lord told the Devil to be quiet. What power we saw as Jesus rebuked the Devil for your sake! Now He has given you the power to enforce on the earth His declaration in that text. Bind it and it is bound, loose it and it is free.

I do not know where you work. It may be an office or school. You may keep a lovely home or work in the church. You may be a Christian minister. I have no idea where the Lord has put you to serve Him, but I know this: you are there to stand in the gap for the lives of those who are around you.

SHARING THE BURDEN

I work in Asia. It is a land filled with idols and ancestral worship. My particular burden is for the Chinese people. Several years ago Wang Ming Dao of Shanghai laid his tortured, withered hands on my head and consecrated me to a work among the Chinese. My life has not been the same since.

In the temples where I work there is the altar of the immortals, and in the back or to the side is the place of the ancestral tablets. On these tablets are inscribed the generations of the Chinese families who pertain to that temple. It is here that offering is made to make a better harmony for departed ancestors.

The worship system involves the Goddess of Mercy and the eight immortals. It is believed they direct the affairs of every Chinese. I have spent days praying over the heads of young men and women who come to seek the will of the goddess. She never speaks. She cannot.

It is through these altars that the generational curses and familiar spirits operate among the clans. It is not unusual to hear curses invoked upon an enemy or to hear dialogue with an ancestor over business matters. Several years ago the Lord led me to "park the ark" in the gap between these altars and the people. I am not praying to the idol, or addressing it in any way. Neither am I lifting up my voice to draw attention to myself in some display of seeming spirituality. In a quiet way I simply stand there and pray in tongues.

When someone prays in an unknown tongue, they speak mysteries unto God (1 Corinthians 14:2). They build themselves up in faith (Jude 20) and they flow in intercession, praying the perfect prayer of the Spirit. As the Lord leads, I bind the familiar spirits of the families of that temple and loose the people to know Jesus as their Lord and Savior. I am happy to report that in the three years in which we have been doing this, the Body of Christ in our test city has doubled.

But, what if you have not yet received the spiritual gift of the baptism in the Holy Spirit with the evidence of speaking in tongues? Can you still be an effective Attack Lamb? Yes, of course you can. It is Jesus in you who is seen by the four forces. It is not the vessel that puts powers to flight, but the One who dwells in you. I encourage you to continue to ask the Lord to give you this very valid gift, but do not disqualify yourself from being the ark just because you do not pray in tongues. Press into Jesus and He will give you all He has for you.

As we stand in the gap and park the ark with the motor running, the evangelist, church planter, outreach coordinators and all the Christian workers are experiencing a great harvest in the city.

As you work in the gap the Lord has given you, you will be effective to loose the people who pertain to that place so they may hear the Gospel and understand it. You will receive from the Lord, through the Holy Spirit, the specific ways to pray and you will hear of souls saved.

Go to that work place as an Attack Lamb and neutralize the power of the four forces. You have been given the freedom to use the Name that is above every name. God has adopted you into His family to direct you into His purpose. He has given you the ability to discern the thoughts and intents of the four forces set against man. He has given you the ability to understand His plan to neutralize their power in every situation, and He has authorized you to use the name of His Son, our Savior Jesus. All that is left for you to do is to convert your place of work to a gap, park the ark, take the key of faith and get your motor running.

CHAPTER 10
Speaking of Names

In the twenty years I have been involved in Christian ministry I have been called many things. Never tall and thin, but many things. My parents were very strong Christians in the Presbyterian church. Father was an elder and Mother played piano, led women's circle groups and taught Sunday School. Our home was, by today's standards, quite strict: short hair, no loud music and morning and evening devotions.

Even as kids we accumulated titles at an early age. We were, of course, in the youth and senior choirs and were expected to shoulder responsibilities in the youth group. As a result, positions and titles were not strangers in our home. We knew how to "do church."

The charismatic movement of the early seventies brought a revision of titles. It still amounted to sincere people doing the service jobs of the church, but now they were called shepherd, undershepherd and so forth. Again I began to accumulate titles. In the twenty-five years I have been involved in charismatic circles, I have been called "Apostle," "Prophet," "Evangelist," "Teacher," and "Pastor." I have been an "Elder," "Deacon," "Home Group Leader," "Worship Leader," and more. By the end of the first fifteen years I had somewhat of an identity crisis. I was called so many things that none of them seemed real. Worse, while I could "do church," I wasn't growing any closer to the Lord.

I sought the Lord concerning this because it seemed to me I should be getting closer, and He led me to the book of Acts.

> **But ye shall receive power, after that the Holy Ghost is come upon you: and ye shall be witnesses unto me both in Jerusalem, and in all Judea, and in Samaria, and unto the uttermost part of the earth.**
>
> **Acts 1:8**

AMAZED

I was amazed. All God had empowered us to be are witnesses. I thought about witnesses. A witness is someone who has seen something happen. He can report only on what he has actually and personally seen. He cannot testify to something someone else has seen. So a witness is someone who has seen something happen, and says what happened.

My immediate question was, "Why do we need the power of the Holy Spirit to be a witness?"

The Lord impressed me with this thought. ***Spiritual work must be done in a spiritual way.*** That's right. The Holy Spirit is the One who reveals to us the things of God. He is the One who knows the deep things of God and shares them with our spirit even to the realization of who we are in Christ. Jesus gives us identity by the power of the Holy Spirit.

Fair enough. As we walk about our place of work, do we not want the Holy Spirit to lead us? As we make decisions and pray in the gaps of our families, don't we want the Holy Spirit to give us faith for their souls? Of course! As we see our own weakness, we want more of the power of the Holy Spirit.

What about the telling? As this witness power descended upon the disciples, they had the experience of speaking in tongues. This was a language they, the ones speaking, did not understand. True, the business men out of every nation heard understandable languages, but when a person speaks in an unknown tongue, he speaks mysteries unto God. A mystery is something **you** do not understand.

I have found that when I think I understand what my heart is telling me to pray, I am often limited or just plain wrong in my feelings. I begin to tell God what I think about the situation from the very limited experience I have. For every one point of which I am certain, there are an infinite number of things about which I know absolutely nothing. I thank God that He has given, through the power of the Holy Spirit, the ability to speak in a language of witness or prayer language that I cannot understand. My tongue can communicate the perceptions of my divinely enabled spirit in a way that I cannot alter through intellect, will, or emotion.

That paragraph had a ton of doctrine in it. Maybe we better chew on that a second. What I am saying is, if I view a situation without the power of the Holy Spirit, I will see it according to or in the light of my own accumulated life experiences. I will process the information and formulate a prayer accordingly.

OPERATING WITH POWER

With the power of the Holy Spirit I look at the same situation, allow it to touch my heart, and pray in tongues, not knowing what the Holy Spirit is communicating. My understanding is unfruitful, but the prayer is most effective. I am not generating the prayer content from a mind that can be affected by what my senses tell me or what I understand of the situation based on past experience. Jesus does not base His work on our lives by what we have been, but on His ability to transform us into what we shall be. In the same sense, prayer in the Spirit impacts the future rather than revisiting the past.

We pray with the Spirit and with the understanding as the apostle Paul directed (1 Corinthians 14:15). As you are standing in your child's room, you may discern the presence of the four forces attempting to keep your child from walking with the Lord. You pray for understanding in the situation. The Lord leads you to pray in an exact fashion by relating thought to your understanding. Certainly we pray in this way with great fruit.

You receive prayer requests through your church prayer chain or through a missions newsletter. You are asked to pray for someone. You begin to pray with the understanding you have received through the phone call or letter. As you pray, you are led into tongues as an avenue of prayer which reaches beyond your understanding. As an Attack Lamb you learn to hear from heaven and to speak those things which the Lord speaks or shows you. You learn not to be locked into one format for prayer, but to flow with the Holy Spirit in the fervent, effectual prayer of those who are made righteous by His blood.

Paul invites us in First Corinthians 14:15 to be flexible and pray in the Spirit and with the understanding. I thank God that He has made a way in which I can pray for thousands of people every day without having to know who they are, where they live, or anything about their lives except that Jesus loves them and that He has brought me to their city to pray for them. Spiritual work must be done in a spiritual way. It is God's will that the four forces be neutralized and people hear the Gospel. We are in the gap asking according to His will. The ark is parked and intercession is being made for all men.

It makes no difference if it is you in your child's room or me on the street in Beijing, the principle is the same. We can pray effectively with the Spirit and with the understanding. Please do not allow the separation of

Pentecostal and Evangelical to keep you from the heavenly vision of all of us gathered before the throne of God making intercession for those who need to be reconciled to Him.

GOING "TRACKING"

I love to pass out tracts; you know, those little booklets designed to tell people about the Lord and lead them to pray to Him. In one three-day period four of us distributed 25,000 tracts hand-to-hand in the country of Nepal. I really like to "go tracking." I have often wondered why in some places people will literally knock you over to get them and in others, they will knock you over to avoid them. The answer is in Acts 1.

Jesus has a certain order to taking a city, region, nation, and the world. He told the disciples to remain at Jerusalem until they were baptized in the Holy Spirit. He wanted this witness power, the ability to see and say, to precede evangelistic outreach. The baptism in the Holy Spirit was, in His instruction, fundamental to evangelism. He did not send out a single Attack Lamb without it.

Can you be Holy Spirit-filled and not speak in tongues? Sure you can. Can you demonstrate the fruit of the Holy Spirit and not speak in tongues? Everyone who has a born-again experience **should** be manifesting the fruit of the Spirit. That is what makes us different from the world. But, the word Jesus said to them was **baptized.**

In Acts 1:8 Jesus tells the disciples **what** they will receive: power. Acts 1:5 tells them **how. "You shall be baptized with the Holy Ghost not many days hence."**

WHAT DOES THIS MEAN?

Jesus was talking about a baptism in the Holy Spirit which was the promise of the Father and was accompanied by these new prayer tongues. Why? So the witness which they would give through the power of the Holy Spirit would release the anointing that caused three thousand men, their wives and kids to come to Christ in one afternoon. In a proven Gospel-resistant culture a former fisherman who had denied Christ stood up in this power and declared the truth. By the same Spirit you too can declare the same truths in the same fashion. Praying in the Spirit is the intercessor's most powerful weapon.

Wow! Can you see people where you work being touched by the power of the Lord because you are praying for them, not according to your feeble knowledge of their lives but in the power of the Holy Spirit, who through you is praying the perfect prayer: that every man woman and child on the face of this earth know that Jesus died for them! I get so excited thinking of you there interceding for your boss, or your teacher, or your family member or just walking through your town in the witness power of the Holy Spirit, gently speaking the mysteries to God.

But, that's not all that is going on. As an Attack Lamb, you have the ability to see a heavenly vision. As you wait in your place of prayer, you can see the purpose of God. You are not distracted by what the Devil is throwing at you, you are focused on the Lamb upon the throne. You give praise as those apostles did in Acts 2.

As you do, the Lord gives you a word for the city, a word for a person, a specific way to pray or prophetic act to do. Now you are seeing heaven and telling earth. This is the second half of witnessing. This is evangelism. You are now involved in what the Lord had intended when he said, **"But wait for the promise of the Father,..."** (Acts 1:4).

TAKING UP YOUR MINISTRY—AND YOUR INHERITANCE

In Psalm 2 we are encouraged, **"Ask of Me and I will give You the nations for Your inheritance and the ends of the earth for Your possession"** (v.8 NKJV). With this witness power came the promise of God, according to His will. Devout men out of every nation were there. He had assembled them together for this great event. The disciples had spent fifty days in prayer waiting for the power of God. When that power came, the results were beyond belief. Every nation was touched. I have been blessed to follow some of the trade routes which people took from that meeting to their homes. All along the way there is documented evidence of the power of the Gospel.

You are now taking up that same ministry. Perhaps you have never felt the presence of this witnessing power. Now is a great time to begin. Lift your thoughts from this page to the Lord. He has called you to see the heavenly vision. You are included through the blood on that mercy seat. He has accepted you in the beloved.

Ask Him now for that witness power and praise Him. As He touches you, He will give you that language you have not spoken before. He will touch you with a prayer language which will be yours alone. Go ahead and declare Jesus as Lord of your life; ask Him to baptize you in the Holy Spirit. We will wait here for you because I do not want you to feel rushed in this. Take your time.

See, here we are in His presence. That was a great prayer time, wasn't it? Just a beginning really as the Lord is equipping this generation of Attack Lambs as He did those who went before us. He loves us so much and wants to pour out great blessings through us to the millions who have yet to know His name. His is a love affair with us.

CHAPTER 11
Cut the Grass

My father loved my mother. My siblings and I grew up in the radiance of that love. We were not wealthy and my father's truck driver's salary did not enable him to give her the beautiful gifts he so much wanted to. He could not afford to buy her fancy crystal vases or flower arrangements, so we filled winter evenings planning our flower beds. We would map out the smallest detail of what would go where, how tall it would grow and what colors would look good together, etc.

Then, at the earliest possible moment, the work would begin. The result was, from early Spring to late Autumn, our yard became a floral display of his undying devotion.

Mother was just as much in love with him. Each evening when he arrived home she presented her love offering to him: a freshly cooked, hot meal of his liking. We children never had the option to decline our father's taste in food. But no matter. Mother would cook wonderful German dishes which filled the house with rich aroma. Our young mouths would water in anticipation. Spetzel was my hands-down favorite.

The garden, which my mother could view from her bedroom window, was of particular importance to my father; it was the tangible measure of his adoration of her. A continual Valentine card in flowers. But there was more than just flowers.

A gray stone walkway was bordered by carefully placed red bricks and then lined with dark topsoil. Meticulous edging, done by hand tools on the grass which grew next to the topsoil, kept a neat, straight line of contrast between the two. Then the grass was cut in patterns, also meticulously. If my father felt a plaid would be nice, or a herring bone, then it was our job to create the sensation with the hand mower and roller, gently bending the blades in his desired expression.

Never did we just fire up a power mower and tear blindly through the grass. After the lawn was mowed, the edges of the grass were trimmed with hand shears so the grass was of uniform height. He was certain to instruct us that gray was gray, red was red, and black was black and green grass clippings did not belong on any of them.

The flowers were set in mulched beds. The deep brown of the mulch gave subtle contrast to the fresh green of the young shoots. Each plant was set in an exact spot according to our winter drawings so as the blooming season progressed, there was a continual cascade of love which my mother observed from the window.

DINNER TIME

The center piece of her table setting was an arrangement of flowers from his offering. Around these were set our six places. Father at the head, my brothers on his left side, Mother at the other head, my sister beside her, and me at my father's right hand.

The table was set to perfection. Each of us children had a day to set it and the precision would make the Sultan's meal look like a microwave special. Fork handles were as specifically placed as marigolds. Plates shown as the petals of her favorite roses. She responded to his love with gleaming joy and pristine passion.

My father arrived home from work each day at the same time, 6:00 P.M. That was the time at which we were expected to be home from our activities, washed, neatly dressed, and ready to enjoy a family meal. We voluntarily ordered our lives around this specific hour. Our respect was made easy by Mother's example. If he was late, there was no bickering; she would take out the double boilers and keep the food at serving temperature until he arrived. We did not eat until he came.

THE LESSON OF A LIFETIME

One Spring Saturday my father woke me very early, just before he left for work, and said, "Cut the grass."

Several hours later when my teenaged eyes finally opened I remembered my friends and I had made big plans for the day. All through the long winter and early spring we had waited for the ball fields to be ready for our baseball games, and the swimming hole water to be warm enough for the daring among us to take the plunge. Today was the day.

I swept through the kitchen, baseball bat in one hand and glove in the other, and had just opened the back door to leave when mother called, "Did your father ask you to cut the grass?"

I was well and truly caught.

Knowing it was futile to attempt escape, I rushed to the garage, got out the mower, never checked to see the pattern, forgot about the edging and the clipping and tore through the grass parts of the garden, leaving a wake of fresh clippings washed ashore on beaches of brown mulch, red brick, and gray walkway. Of course I finished in record time. I grabbed up my glove and bat and dashed off with my friends to an afternoon of baseball and swimming.

I arrived home at 5:30 in anticipation of our 6:00 feast. The aroma of mother's offering was spectacular. The gentle breeze carried its sweet savors into the whole neighborhood and embraced me while still far from home. We were having spetzles.

Spetzles are these little dumplings unique to the Bavarian homeland of our family. They are more than wonderful. My father, brothers and I would always bet to see who could eat the most. We could pack away bushels of spetzles. Then we would all sit back in our chairs and tell Mother how great that batch was and pat our stomachs and enjoy the moment of sheer gluttony.

Passing through the kitchen I verified that we were about to consume my favorite meal. I could taste it as I washed and put on a clean shirt. My mouth was watering as I went to my place at the table. I had to sit on my hands to keep from sampling the feast before me.

My father had arrived from work. I heard the sound of the car as it entered the drive way. His voice was pleasant as he called to my mother. I heard the familiar sounds as he washed off the grime of another day on the road and heard the steady pace of his footfall as he climbed the steps to the living area.

Their greeting was always the same. He smiled at her and she came to him and they gave a little peck. They never embraced in front of the children, but the intensity of their eyes set the standard for each of our marriages. He then checked the stove top and expressed his appreciation for her labor of love.

A LESSON LEARNED

When Father came into the dining room it was our signal to assemble. We four children never had to be called a second time. From my place at his right hand I watched the others as they came to the table. Each one had been involved in something but dropped it immediately when my father signaled that the time had come. Our worlds revolved around his timing.

We joined hands and he prayed. It was the same at every dinner I can remember. He always humbled himself and our family to acknowledge Jesus as our Savior and Provider. My left hand disappeared in the giant gentleness of his right hand. The strength of that bond was to hold me to Christ for all time.

With the close of prayer, he continued to hold my hand and said, "You may leave the table."

I was in shock. The blood drained from my face and breath came in gasps. The flood of anticipation in my mouth was replaced by a desert of despair. A waterfall of emotion began to gather behind rapidly blinking eyelids and I looked to my mother for support. She was very busy dishing out long-anticipated servings to my sister.

"Sir?" It was more a plea for time than an attempt to respond.

"You may leave the table," he repeated.

The repeated instruction gave me no more information than the original. I didn't understand.

My eyes flew to my brother's faces for some clue as to what the problem could be, and for any kind of help they could offer. Whether it was the tone of his voice or the realization they were going to get to eat my share of spetzles that caused them to look away I cannot be sure, but one thing was certain, they were not going to get involved.

"May I ask why?" I squeaked out.

My question caused complete silence. I think the world stood still for an eternity. I know our home did.

"I told you to cut the grass."

His voice was steady, secure, non-negotiable. He knew he was just and right in his decision. He said no more.

I knew he was right as well. He had asked me to do just one thing and I had not done it. He was not being cruel, he was right. I had broken relationship. The silence was devastating as I slipped from my chair and went slowly to my room.

Mother did not bring me any food that evening. There was no grace in this. We were taught to obey our father or pay the price, and she was not going to undermine that teaching in any way. When she was asked why, she told us she felt she owed it to our future wives to make good husbands for them.

It was the lesson of my life. I have never forgotten it, and it has motivated me when nothing else could.

JESUS SAID...

Our Lord and Saviour has similarly given us a command, our own "Cut the grass." Jesus said, **"...All authority has been given to Me in heaven and on earth. Go therefore and make disciples of all the nations,..."** (Matthew 28:18,19 NKJV). The command is simple, "Go."

Our going out is based not on the need of the world, but on the authority of the Lamb upon the throne. He said "Go." It is commonly understood that to go one must get up from where he is and move in some direction toward a new location. People ask me to pray for them and give them a "word of direction." They want me to tell them where the Lord wants them to go so if they have a hard time they don't have to take responsibility for the decision. They can blame it on me or, worse yet, God speaking through me.

I won't do it. The first law of direction is motion. For centuries the Church has sat in one place and said, "Lord, direct us." That is like a child pretending to drive a car. Until the thing moves there is no point in asking for direction.

Jesus has already said, "Go." That is very plain. Because He knew we wouldn't want to hear it, He wrote it down. In the Greek it says, "Go." In other words, get into motion. Everyone in the Bible is in motion. Abraham, Isaac, Jacob all moved about. David, Jesus, Paul, they all moved about. In fact, the one time David did not go out when he should have, he got into sin with the girl next door.

THE CHARISMATIC "MOVEMENT"

If you want to know where all the sin came from in the charismatic movement, consider this. It wasn't a movement because the people never went anywhere.

They all played games, swam in streams of anointing and had a great feel-good time, but they never did the one thing Jesus said to do. They never cut the grass. The two-thirds of the world which has yet to hear the name of Jesus in a way it can understand is evidence to a just God of the rebellion of His people.

Yes, they were baptized in the Holy Spirit. Yes, more money flowed than ever has in the history of the Church. Yes, great buildings were built. Yes, great music was written. Yes, there are more books and book stores than ever in the history of the Church. But the unharvested fields are still standing there. The uncut grass stands there, a silent witness.

The fields are still ripe unto harvest and the Church is still playing games and looking for a fresh pool to plunge itself into. Jesus **is** coming back. When He gets here, the grass had better be cut or there are going to be some pretty shocked people leaving the table.

UNDER COMMAND

Jesus has made you an Attack Lamb. His plan is to put intercessors on every corner of the land and neutralize the Enemy's four forces through His Power Presence. He said, **"Go...and, lo, I am with you alway,..."** (Matthew 28:19,20). We have the ability to use His Name which is above all names. We go in His authority. He has given us the power to witness, the ability to see and say. Now, the choice is ours. Will you do it?

As we read on I will share with you the five pressure points that will change a nation. I'll teach you what to do when you park the ark and why it is important to keep that motor running in the spirit. But you must decide to go on. Will you make the choices that align you with God's purpose on earth?

I believe you will join the millions world wide who have said to the Lord, "Jesus, I am sorry that I have lived so much for myself. I give my life to You. Lead me in paths of righteousness for Your Name's sake. Redirect the affairs of my life that I may respond to Your love for me. I accept Your love offering of the nations, and will enter in with You to Your inheritance."

There, now can't you just smell that dinner?

CHAPTER 12

𝒲𝒶𝓇

We had come to Moscow on the train from Beijing. Our trip had been a real eye-opener. We had gotten off the train in several places: Ulan Battur, Irkutsk and Novosibirsk. We were now focused on the seat of power for the communist regime.

Now I found myself walking through the Kremlin asking the Lord for a strategy to free the Soviet people. It was 1985 and the USSR was in full bloom.

For two days I sat in the replica of Lenin's office and practiced the Power Presence of the Holy Spirit. I asked the Lord for insight into the power of the *archas* which was emanating from that place. "What," I asked, "would break the power of the lie that there is no God?" The Lord impressed me that the word of truth would break that power.

From Lenin's office, I walked the two blocks to his tomb. Rather than join the line to enter the tomb, I took up a location opposite the front door. I began to softly declare, "There is a God. He has a Son. His Name is Jesus. He died for Me." I walked about the entire Kremlin complex repeating this same declaration. Each time I repeated those phrases I experienced a greater sense of freedom.

For the next few days I stood in the Kremlin garden, an Attack Lamb on location, and softly spoke the declaration, "There is a God. He has a Son. His name is Jesus. He died for me." All too soon our scheduled time ended and it was time to move on.

For the next several years whenever we went prayer walking in parts of the Soviet Union or sent teams there, we continued to make this gentle, confident declaration. We mobilized Attack Lambs from Beijing to Berlin, and today the former Soviet Union walks in more religious freedom than it has in decades. The simple declaration of the Word of God's truth established the reality of what we declared.

AN OPEN DECLARATION

We have declared war on the Devil's four forces. We are determined to touch every nation according to the command of our Lord and Leader Jesus, and to do it according to His plan. And as we do, one thing we know for sure. We are not wrestling with flesh and blood. We are wrestling with four concentrations of power. They were defeated in heaven, defeated on the earth, and defeated under the earth. The disciples reported that in the power Jesus gave them, the four forces voluntarily ordered themselves under the name of Jesus. It's our job to enforce that victory.

We have seen, as we are faithful to the purpose of God in the earth, these four forces can be neutralized since we have the same power the disciples had. We can share their experience. The four forces are no match for an Attack Lamb parked in front of a Dagon of today, and as long as we are living to present Jesus to every man, woman, and child on the earth in our generation, it will ever be so.

OUR NEXT ACROSTIC

In the next three chapters, we are going to follow this acrostic...**WAR**.

WORSHIP
ANNOUNCE
REJOICE

All successful spiritual endeavor comes forth from an attitude of **worship.** When the disciples returned to the Lord in Luke 10, they reported to Jesus that even the devils were subject to them in Jesus' name. After centuries of bondage in the nation, this was incredibly good news. Jesus declared they had authority over all the power of the Enemy, and that nothing would in any way harm them. Sounds like a pretty secure war zone to me.

As fabulous as that truth was, and still is, Jesus responded by making one of the most startling replies of His entire ministry. He called them to a priority of focus. He commanded them to rejoice not in who was submitted to them, but rather, to rejoice in Him to whom they were submitted.

If we depart from a focus on Jesus and begin to focus on the forces which oppose us, we give them a place they are not entitled to.

How about the one who prays and rejoices in Jesus? They are filled with joy, and rather than focus on the works of evil, they overcome evil with good.

20/20 VISION IN THE 10/40 WINDOW

The 10/40 Window is the part of the world in which are found the least evangelized, mega-people groups. If they are to be reached, Attack Lambs are going to have to go forth and "park the ark" with the motor running until the Dagons of today bow down, releasing the people to hear the name of Jesus.

Second Chronicles 20:1 illustrates how King

115

Jehoshaphat faced the challenge of the children of Ammon, Moab, and Mount Seir, using power worship as an instrument of warfare.

The Moabites, the Ammonites and those from Mount Seir have come against Jehoshaphat to do battle. The war was on! These peoples, conceived through incest, are the descendents of Lot and his daughters. The same forces the Lord engaged in battle at Sodom and Gomorrah are now at it again.

In this case, those forces are the *pneuma tae ponerias* and the *archas* combination. How do we know? The history of sexual perversion tells the tale of malice. Sexual perversion destroys the individual. It corrupts body, soul, and spirit. According to Romans 1 it will render the mind incapable of rational thought. First Corinthians 6 says it will cost you your ability to function in the kingdom of God and, worst of all, it will cause spiritual union with the Enemy.

Those who entice and involve others in corrupt sexual practices are malicious in nature. They are driven by a spirit of malice, which is a Dagon of today. You and I have the power of God's presence to stand in quiet confidence and see them bow down. When the children of sexual impurity solicit our families, we can stand in the gap. Our victory is assured if we stand in faith. We can lift our hearts and eyes to a heavenly vision, and see the glory flow from the throne, as we declare victory over the Devil's forces.

The war-loving "*archas* of Seir," who likes to ride upon the high places and intimidate, is the force King Jehoshaphat has to battle. The sexually impure love to intimidate the rest of society saying, "We will get your daughters and sons for our pleasures."

In America today there is a spiritual movement accusing 98% of the population of having a fear of homosexuals. Two percent is saying to ninety-eight percent, "You are afraid of us!" That is ridiculous! It is the same ploy attempted by the demons who try to get you to forget there were two angels who remained obedient to God for every one who did not. The implied superiority of evil is fed through the force of the *archas*. We wrestle with this force for the salvation of others.

FOCUS, KING JEHOSHAPHAT, FOCUS

Now these two forces have come up against King Jehoshaphat. In verse three he finds his proper focus,

And Jehoshaphat feared, and set himself to seek the Lord, and proclaimed a fast throughout all Judah. And Judah gathered themselves together, to ask help of the Lord: even out of all the cities of Judah they came to seek the Lord.

2 Chronicles 20:3-4

Proper focus in time of trouble is demonstrated by the king, and all those who followed him. They did three things necessary for victory.

First, they set themselves to seek the Lord. They did not look to neighboring armies for help. They did not appoint a committee but became a prayer group to handle this. They all sought God. Every person looked for a heavenly vision.

Second, they fasted. They denied their appetite for things of earth to create a greater appetite for the Lord. They turned off their senses to seek His face. Through fasting, they sealed off the Enemy's access to them. In all times of warfare there is special training to prepare the warriors. Fasting is vital to successful spiritual warfare.

Third, they gathered together. The way of the world is separation, and Satan's strategies often include isolation. Hitler, Stalin, Kruschev, and Mao are the most recent examples of leadership developing exclusive rather than inclusive practice. It is through this exclusive attitude that the *archas* invades the hearts of nations.

"Not forsaking the assembling of ourselves to-

gether, as the manner of some is;..." (Hebrews 10:25) was not written to insure a large attendance or a large offering. It is the directive of the Holy Spirit, knowing that as we gather together Jesus is present in the midst of us, and His wisdom and power will be manifest. By gathering together, these people affirmed their faith in the king and his direction to fast and seek God. They rallied to the call of leadership. They were faithful to the principle of submission.

ATTACK LAMB INTERCESSION

Jehoshaphat's prayer of 2 Chronicles 20:1-12 contains several very important lessons about Attack Lamb intercession.

First, he stood in the midst of the people before the new court of the temple to pray. He was in the gap. He was between the people and the Lord in a position to make sacrifice if the problem was the sin of the people. He did not lord his kingship over them, but **identified with them**.

Isaiah was in a similar position when he said, **"Woe is me!...I am a man of unclean lips, and I dwell in the midst of a people of unclean lips:..."** (Isaiah 6:5). He identified with the people in their sinful state.

Paul was identifying with the prisoners as he called out to the jailor not to kill himself saying, "We are all here." This principle of identifying with the people is vital to the ministry of intercession. We cannot stand aloof from the crowd to avoid being touched in our hearts with their sin. Remember, we too have fallen short of the glory of God at times.

As a witness you have the ability, through the Holy Spirit, to identify with the sinner in the consequence of sin without becoming a doer of that sin. You do not have to do drugs to feel the pain of the drug addict. If you are willing to walk among the lepers, God will allow you to pray until their pain lifts. You will feel as much as He allows to keep you in prayer.

I have often experienced the feeling of total helplessness of the Buddhist as he stands before an image that cannot see, hear, or touch him and cries out for his ancestors. My identification with the ethnic Chinese grows in depth each time I stand and pray for them. So by the grace of God I am no longer a foreigner in their midst.

Jesus became our sin. Through this experience, He is touched with our infirmities. His heart is our heart. His feelings our feelings. He bore our griefs and carried our sorrows. And now, He ever lives to make intercession for us. He is still identified with you. When He moves in your life, He causes you to have the grace to identify with those for whom you are praying. You are not alone in the gap.

Second, King Jehoshaphat proclaims who God is. His proclamation in verses six and seven establishes that God has brought them to this point in time, and dwells among them. It is vital to success as a leader that we **maintain the focus** of those around us on the fact of the sovereignty of God. Should the people look to us, the enemy, or themselves, we are headed for disaster. The king directs the attention of the people to the person of God.

Third, he **declares the promise** of God. Look in verse 9 at the power of this declaration, **"If, when evil cometh...we stand before this house,...and cry unto thee...then you will hear and help."** What strength there is in the promise of God. What comfort there is in His presence. What joy in the realization of His Person.

Fourth, he **reminds the Lord** that the entire situation is the result of a sovereign decision made at the time Israel came up into the land. Moab and Ammon exist because God had given orders not to destroy them. He had been giving them time to repent. He is faithful to the heart of Abraham concerning Lot. The power of intercession has kept these people in the mercy of the Lord for generations, but now they are showing their true nature and will be judged.

Fifth, verse thirteen describes the scene as all

Israel stands before the Lord. Men, women, and children have been fasting and seeking the Lord together. **Prayer is a family affair**. There is unity of purpose as together they call on God to defend them from the attack of their ungrateful enemy. The king leads in prayer with the agreement of the people. In their act of submission to him, and to God through him, they release the power of His presence, which will cause their enemies to submit.

GOD RESPONDS

By His Spirit, God speaks through one of the young men. He is Jahaziel whose name means "Beheld of God." He is the son of Zechariah, "The Lord Remembers," who is the son of Benaniah, "The Lord has Built Up," who is the son of Jeil, "Jehovah Sweeps Away," the son of Mattaniah, "The Gift of Yahweh," who is a Levite, "Joined to Yahweh," of the sons of Asaph, "The Gatherer." The names are very important as the Lord speaks directly, and not through an ephod or Urim and Thummim.

To those gathered together, the names became their confirmation as this young man speaks direction to king and priest alike. Imagine how the night would have gone without this confirmation. They would question his youth. His family, his position, and his spirituality would all be topics of conversation as they waited throughout that night. Imagine how the generals would feel when he said there would be no need to fight in this battle. How would those who had faced combat prepare for a nation threatening invasion if they did not have the confirmation of the names?

The Lord speaks to His people. They are not without direction. They have sought Him and He is found of them. He has responded to their prayer and fasting, their unity, and their submission. He gives them clear directive, **"Be not afraid nor dismayed by reason of this great multitude; for the battle is not yours, but God's."** (2 Chronicles 20:15).

God agrees with Jehoshaphat. He has allowed these aggressive people to flourish at this time but He will take care of them. Judah has found herself in the midst of the conflict between God and the sons of Lot. The people are in the gap interceding for the will of God to be done.

God has been trying to reach Ammon and Moab since the deliverance of their father Lot. Israel has been brought to the position of prayer through the sovereign nature of God, and their prayers have been Spirit-led. They have chosen to fight the battle in the spiritual dimension, and not in the flesh, and, in so doing have released the very presence of God to war in their behalf.

They have become...Attack Lambs!

THE BATTLE IS THE LORD'S

God tells them when and where to find the gap. In the morning they are to go to a cliff at the river's end. God issues the daily orders; there are three. He commands them to "set themselves," "stand still," and "see their salvation." These commands are our orders as well when we bring our ark into the presence of the Dagons of today.

Here is the verse as a whole and then we will break them down.

> **Ye shall not need to fight in this battle: set yourselves, stand ye still, and see the salvation of the Lord with you, O Judah and Jerusalem: fear not, nor be dismayed; tomorrow go out against them: for the Lord will be with you.**
>
> **2 Chronicles 20:17**

Set yourself. Israel has proven their ability to be in location, in prayer and fasting, with a proper focus. The families stand together and the nation stands behind their leader. They have a proper focus and are not wandering about between opinions.

Stand still. Wow! Do people have a difficult time

121

doing this. "Don't just stand there, do something!" is a common challenge to people today. We feel physical activity is a sign of life and vitality. Once you are in the gap, there is no need for a lot of activity.

Two of my team and I had gone to a Buddhist temple in Singapore in the midst of a Lunar New Year's celebration to intercede for the families who pertain to that temple. I had positioned myself in a gap, literally, between the people and the altar, and softly mentioned the name of Jesus repeatedly.

Along side the altar was what was called a "Money Tree." It was a huge urn over six feet across and six feet high, resting on a broad flat bottom and filled with soil. A small tree rose from the large urn, and people pinned money to it as offerings to the Buddha.

For an hour I remained in the gap softly mentioning the name of Jesus when, suddenly, this huge urn simply fell over, crashing into the altar.

We were in shock!

The Singaporeans in our team felt the controlling spirit of the temple and the city had actually bowed down to the name of Jesus.

The temple workers were even more shocked. There was no natural explanation for how the urn could even tip, let alone fall completely over. There had been no one even near it. The workers scrambled to gather the little packets of money which had been affixed to the tree and, in complete disbelief, called for help to set it upright.

There is power in the presence of the Lord in your life, and in the lives of those for whom you intercede. Stand still and trust in Him; He will cause the powers about you to submit. Let's turn that old adage around...Don't just do something, STAND THERE!

See the salvation. Stand in that gap with a heavenly vision. Be a witness in the power of the Holy Spirit. As you stand in your assigned gap you are going to have opportunity to look at the enemy, his forces, yourself, your weakness, your leadership, their weaknesses, those who stand around you, and their weaknesses. Keep your eyes on the heavenly vision! It is awesome to watch God deliver the Enemy into your hands.

AN INTERNATIONAL MINISTRY

Prayer walking has become an international ministry. There are prayer teams walking in every country. Now they are pressing in on specific people groups. The path of world evangelism has been defined by ethnicity. Any political entity may contain thousands of ethnic or people groups.

The Enemy is using this redefinition to set man against man in bloody conflict once again. The cry of the Enemy is preeminence. Bosnians say the land is theirs, Serbs say they were there first. The term "ethnic cleansing" covers the *ponerias*-driven mass murders of these times. These ethnic *archas-ponerias* combinations are throughout all the earth trying to distract people from the real conflict between God and the Devil. As we walk in the highways and byways of the earth, we bring peace because we are doing battle where the real warfare is manifest and accomplished: in the spiritual realm.

As an Attack Lamb, you are being used of the Lord to release the Power Presence of God. It is His presence alone that tears down the walls which divide the ethnic groups and cause such hatred. Only Jesus can cause man to love man.

BACK TO THE STORY

King Jehoshaphat hears the Word of the Lord from Jahaziel (2 Chronicles 20:17) and falls on his face. The Levites jump and sing and shout. Of these two responses to the presence of the Lord which is correct? We are living in times when the Spirit of God is manifesting in many places with a message of peace and joy. Some places people laugh hysterically. In others the people sit quietly and in others they fall over and are in ecstasy for minutes and hours appearing to be disoriented. Just as these groups in 2 Chronicles 20:18 responded differently, there are differing responses today to the presence, power, and promise of God.

Both groups are right. You cannot evaluate the presence of the Lord by people's response to Him. Their response, however, is critical. Do they embrace the Word of the Lord as truth and act accordingly?

In fact, that is what they do. In the morning they head out in an order which the king has determined after talking with the people. He sends the psalmists first. Not coincidentally, this places the young man with the Word from God right in the front row, and puts the king in the middle with the generals.

The praisers are focused on the beauty of His holiness, and they are given a song to sing, "Praise the Lord, for His mercy is forever." They do not just mill about humming whatever comes to mind. They have a definite position, a definite responsibility and a definite song.

Here is where the process of **announcement** begins. Remember our acrostic **W-A-R**. Everyone does not do what seems good to them, but it is a very disciplined march.

What happened? God gave the victory. He sets ambushments against the three armies, and they turn inward and attack each other. The preeminent arrogance of the *archas* and the treachery of the *ponerias* combine, and they destroy each other while the Attack Lambs stand and sing a very simple song.

I believe if the Body of Christ would be positive, move in the calling God has for us to step into gaps at pressure points, and do as Judah did, the forces which drive Hinduism, Buddhism and Islam would turn against each other and the masses who live under those systems would be released to know Jesus as their Lord and Savior. This is the will of God.

WINNING YOUR BATTLES

Do not argue with your family, your classmate, your colleague. **We do not wrestle with flesh and blood**. Our battle is with spiritual forces, the Dagons of today. As we move into the 10/40 window toward the least evangelized, mega-peoples, it will be hours of prayer and fasting that will get the job done. The four forces, *archas, exousias, kosmokratos,* and *ponerias* will be broken from them, just as they were in Jehoshaphat's day, and multiplied millions will come to know Jesus.

The action taken in 2 Chronicles 20 has five distinguishing characteristics:

> It was Spirit-led.
> It was leader-affirmed.
> It included all the people.
> It was gift ordered, praisers first etc.
> It was God's battle.

When the strategy for taking your city has the same characteristics, you will experience the same great victory.

Take the time to compare your prayer plans with this one. How do they line up? Here are some questions you can ask yourself to see.

Are you open to the Holy Spirit showing you the way He wants you to go?

Has your leadership authorized your going forth, or are you trying to make the forces submit without submitting yourself?

Are you including as many people in the plan as possible?

Do you allow gifted people other than yourself to be in the front or do you insist on having that place? (Watch out for the *archas* if you feel you must be in front.)

Finally, have you taken the promise of success to the cross?

Promised victory is pretty heady stuff. If it is God's battle, then give Him the glory. Keep your focus on Jesus. Keep your vision in the heavenlies.

The environment of the throne room is praise and worship. It is not a war room, it is a victory celebration. Judah went forth in an atmosphere of praise and worship. Remember: **all conclusive battles are won with praise and worship because the Godward focus of a submitted people releases the Power Presence of God from which the Enemy must flee in absolute confusion.**

Give the report to the people of the Lord, "Your warfare is accomplished. The Four Forces are subject to us as we walk in God's ordered praise and worship. Tell it in Zion and declare it to Jerusalem: there is victory in the name of the Lord!"

CHAPTER 13

And Again I Say Rejoice

Three thousand hands clapping full force filled the renovated theater in Singapore with noise. Thunderous applause would describe it. The people had leapt to their feet in one motion. Their voices rode the thunder with shouts of joy, and tears of release cascaded over upturned cheeks. Their smiles stretched away wrinkles of fear as the Holy Spirit gave them a heavenly vision.

They were free. Man had not done it. Programs had not done it. Jesus had touched them through the power of His presence and they would never be the same.

Time stood still. Its usual hectic control of their lives was cast aside as minute after minute was consumed in the ecstasy of their release. The walls echoed their joy sending waves of thanksgiving crashing in crescendo with their barrier-breaking bellows.

The pastor stood before them, hands raised in surrender, and his eyes closed to earthly sights. His spirit was open to heaven's throne as he waited while the Savior of these souls delivered them from generations of bondage. He had just testified that the force of intimidation had been broken. Now in his first moments of freedom, he rolled his shoulders as if to test the new garment of righteousness with which the Spirit had draped him. More than a mantle, this was an anointing to set the captive free.

A young lady came forward. Unafraid, she took a position near a microphone, yet she would not be able to speak for a quarter hour as the people continued to rejoice in victory. Arms aching, hands swelling from the pounding hand clapping, voices hoarse from shouting, they carried on. The power was not theirs. They rode with Christ upon the thunder of their praise. They were seated with Him in the chariot of God far above powers and principalities.

At last, as their bodies returned to the limits of humanity, they listened as the young lady reported, "Each time a hand clap sounded another demon of intimidation was driven from a Singaporean. Each clap released another soul from bondage." The roar began again.

DECLARATION OF TRIUMPH

Rejoicing, the "R" in **W-A-R**, is the declaration of triumph in the Lord Jesus. Paul writes to the Philippians to **"Rejoice in the Lord alway: and again I say, Rejoice"** (Philippians 4:4). How was it that Paul and Silas had been able to rejoice that night in a jail cell? They had a heavenly vision. They knew they were a part of God's plan to reach the lost. Until their last breath, they were going to announce to powers and principalities the victory that was theirs, and ours, in Jesus.

As he taught the church, Paul emphasized the power of rejoicing. He knew it to be a release point for the Power Presence of God. The earth had shaken and, when it did the jailor and his family had come into the kingdom of God. Rejoicing power had brought them from a life of death to a life without death. They were baptized and embraced the apostles, finally sending them to other unreached groups with the Good News. The power of rejoicing had taken Paul and Silas a long way.

It is the will of God that none should perish, but that all should come to the knowledge of the Truth. The angels in heaven rejoice over one sinner who repents. As you stand in that gap and pray, the angels are getting ready to party. They know this works. They know that rejoicing is a big part of successful spiritual endeavor for it is a part of worship, and all successful spiritual endeavor comes from an attitude of praise and worship.

LIFE IN THE STREET

As we walk through the nations of Asia, we realize when the rain falls, we all get wet. To people in the streets, life's showers are a common experience. There is a sort of humor we share with the people as the rains of monsoon turn the streets into rivers. Asian people love to see without being seen.

In Hanoi, Vietnam, there is a shopping district whose winding streets are lined with shops. Displays of wares have spilled out past the sidewalk barriers into the street. At regular intervals the local police come to clear a path through the mountains of plastic and cottons. Stacks of television sets yield to their cane batons. Sharp, Panasonic, and Sony all cry out. But after the authorities pass on, the vendors go back to displaying their goods as much as they can.

But at mid-afternoon the real equalizer moves in, the afternoon monsoon rains. Instantly this kaleidoscope of colors and goods is interrupted by a deluge. The big show is on. There is a mad dash to the plastic awnings in front of their shops. Vendors grab merchandise and hustle it to the safety of cover. We stand under whatever cover can be found and begin to congratulate those who make the many trips to reach common shelter. Each soul who reaches our ship of dryness is greeted with applause and the warm, gracious smiles of the Vietnamese people. Rejoicing together in the simple comfort of covering we share, we are, for the moment, friends. It lasts until the rain quits and then, still strangers in the larger arena, we go back into the now cooler streets.

There is no rejoicing that can compare with that of a freshly pressed and prim school girl who, upon reaching the cover of that shelter, realizes her hair is not going to be destroyed after all, and her skirt pleats are still quite in order. We all wait for the rejoicing outburst as school friends gather under cover and, as surely as the rain itself, they burst into the giggles which let the observer know they have been found out. Adults look to one another and smiles of joy replace scowls of complaint.

You are sent forth as Attack Lambs to proclaim spiritual shelter to those who are caught in the deluge of life's cares. Give yourself to those people. Allow your spirit to be touched with the plight of their Christless lives. See the despair in their eyes as the thunder sounds. Get into that gap and put up a shelter of His Power Presence. Give them the chance to turn away from the torrents of pressure and floods of concern and find refuge in the shelter of the Lord's Presence.

THE HORSE AND RIDER

As the conquistadors attacked the Incas, those smaller, indigenous peoples ran for caves and crevasses. The Spaniard was so large, more than ten feet tall with four hoofed feet and two heads. The larger head had flared nostrils and blood streaked eyes. It was larger than a man's, and its neck thrust forth from a powerful chest.

The smaller head was covered with metal that stones and spears could not penetrate. Fire burst out of one hand as the smaller head looked toward them. The searing pain of the fire would take the life from them.

Incan warriors attacked the unprotected larger head and, in fact, found that if they struck it in just the right spot with club, spear or arrow they could knock it down. However, the smaller-headed portion would rise up and the fire would still come out of its arm and take the life out of their bodies. Eventually, they learned the horse and rider were two and not one. Unfortunately, this discovery came after they had been conquered.

Only the Lord has the answer for both the horse and the rider. Exodus 15 is Moses' great song of rejoicing for the children of Israel who have found shelter in the presence of the Lord. The pillar warmed them by night and the cloud cooled them by day and they were able to witness the great deliverance as the horse and the rider of Pharaoh's armies were cast into the sea.

Moses has seen the fruit of his intercession. He was the first one to spend forty years in the wilderness, preparing to go back to Egypt to stand in the gap for Israel. It was he who declared himself unfit for service. It was he who said he was not eloquent. It was he who had to have the help of his brother, and who cried out to God as he suffered the rejection of the people for whom he interceded.

It was Moses who engaged in spiritual warfare as the Lord performed the ten miracles of deliverance. It was Moses who withstood the treachery of Pharaoh's magicians, Jannes and Jambres. It was Moses who saw the power of God. Now, at the mid-point of his ministry of intercession, it is he who sings this song of rejoicing, **"...I will sing unto the Lord, for he hath triumphed gloriously: the horse and his rider hath he thrown into the sea"** (Exodus 15:1). Not just the horse, and not just a thrown rider. The victory over the Enemy is complete! Both the horse and rider are cast into the sea. Moses has seen the greatest deliverance of all time. They are drowned; they are defeated! Praise the Lord!

HORSES AND RIDERS TODAY

If I say to you, "Communism is the horse," who is the rider? Think about it. The lie of communism is, "There is no God." That is the way in which the State takes the place of God in the society. So communism is the horse on which atheism rides.

If I say to you, "Hinduism is the horse," who is the rider? The Hindu embraces several hundred million gods. Polytheism is the rider of the Hindu horse. We wrestle not with the peoples of Hindu lands. They are precious, wonderful people for whom Christ died, but the horse and the rider are thrown into the sea as we rejoice.

If I say to you, "Buddhism is the horse," who is the rider? The followers of Buddha believe there is no heavenly reward. There are reincarnations, but all of the hereafter is spent in another life form in the here and now. So the rider is the lie, "No heaven." Hear the song of John Lennon after marrying a Buddhist, "Imagine there's no heaven, it's easy if you try..."[1]

I rejoice daily as I walk and work in Asia that the horse and the rider have been thrown into the sea. Not just the religious system, but the spirit behind it all is defeated through the blood of Jesus. As we go to our points of prayer, park the ark, praise the Lord, gain His perception, and pray with His Power Presence, we too shall see horses and riders worldwide fall into the sea and be defeated.

Permit me one more example. If I say to you, "Islam is the horse," who is the rider? Is it not the false prophet who denies the virgin birth, the miracles of Christ, the fulfillment of Abraham, and the death and bodily resurrection of the Son of God? Do we wrestle with the horse? No. Do we wrestle with the people under this dominion? No. We wrestle with the *archas* and *exousias* which operate through this system. We go to strategic locations and call upon the Lord.

Standing in the shade of the same cloud with the

heat of the same fire, we speak to the *archas, exousias, kosmokratos*, and *ponerias* which operate in these places. We maintain God's Power Presence, and see the souls of men delivered. We sing with Moses, **"...I will sing unto the Lord, for he hath triumphed gloriously: the horse and his rider hath he thrown into the sea"** (Exodus 15:1).

IS IT WORKING?

We were recently in a city in western China. Our team had been praying up from Pakistan, and had come through the mountains on the Old Silk Road. The team was walking about in a mosque when one of the teachers invited them to come in and visit. They did and upon entry, this old man closed the door securely behind him and asked in earnest, "Did you bring it with you?"

Quite uneasy, the leader responded, "Did we bring what?"

"The Gospel," the old man replied. "We have been praying for five years that someone would bring us the Gospel." This man knew the sound of the horse; for him it was Buddhism. He knew the emptiness of the rider; no heaven. He had heard from the radio the good news of Jesus Christ and had been praying for five years that someone would bring him the book of the One whose Word is true! Because we had agreed to step into that gap, we were allowed to be the ones to bring it to him.

The world is waiting for you to put on your Attack Lamb mentality and get out there. Do not fear the horses. Do not worry about the riders. God is in control. Give your life over to Him and join in the victory song. The horse and the rider are thrown into the sea!

Think it through. How many horse and rider combinations can you perceive in your community or place of work? In the USA it has been thirty years since the Lord's Prayer was declared illegal in schools. Many efforts have been mounted to restore prayer, but to no avail. Many horses have been slain, but the rider has yet to be destroyed. Can you think of situations in which you have been unsuccessful in unseating the rider?

Ask the Lord to show you the instances in which you have been successful in neutralizing the power of the horse, only to have your hopes dashed as you realize the rider is still at work. List each one. Pray that the Lord will show you how they work together. Remember, you are not to get involved in struggles with people. Behind each of these combinations you will find one or more of the four forces set against salvation.

ROCK MUSIC...REALLY?

Five-tone rock music is often the repetition of musical scales which have their root in Hindu or Buddhist chants to invoke spirits. These repeated scales were learned by the pioneers of rock music during their sojourns to the East. The sounds were novel and sold a lot of records. However, they brought with them their accompanying spiritual riders. Just as the Lord dwells in the praises of His people, demonic forces dwell in these rhythmic progressions.

Many parents have become heartsick at the changes in their children as they open their spirits and minds to these songs. The kids say that they don't even hear the lyrics, they just like the music. When the parents attempt to regain control, frustration sets in and they become angry. Well, guess what? That is exactly the point of the music. Music from Japan is used to invoke Shinto spirits of anger, and music from India is used to invoke Kali, the god of destruction, of the Hindu people.

The result is global. The horse is controlled but the rider is killing the kids. This is the number one weapon the Enemy is using against young people. How are you, the ark of the covenant, going to stop this onslaught on your home? Through the power of rejoicing.

The first proclamation of a worshiping warrior is, "The Devil is defeated." Jesus defeated him in the heavens. He has defeated him on the earth. Jesus has defeated the Devil under the earth. Jesus is Lord! This proclamation defeats the work of the Enemy in three areas.

It defeats the *archas* through the declaration of the preeminence of Christ. He alone is before all things. By Him all things consist. It pleased the Father that in Christ all fullness should dwell (Colossians 1:19). There is no room for the Enemy or any other disorderly, rebellious thing. Jesus has established order and since you are born again, you are a part of that order. You have been set in a position in Christ which is far above all *archas* and *exousias*. You are the righteousness of God in Christ Jesus, the head and not the tail. You have authority over all the power of the Devil (Luke 10:19).

The *archas* cannot intimidate you. It cannot tell you that you are going to lose your child or friend to the ways of the world. You have the agreement of heaven for the salvation and maturation of that soul. You have lived a witness. You have trained up that child. Do not throw away your joy because of a few months of difficulty, reach out to that kid and tell them you love them. The *archas* is not in control of your life or of the lives of those who pertain to you.

Paul told the Philippian jailor, **"Believe on the Lord Jesus Christ, and you will be saved, you and your household"** (Acts 16:31 NKJV)

The jailor did a brilliant thing, he took the ark home with him. He did not leave his new-found friends at the jail, he took them home. He brought God's Power Presence into his home. Bring it in to yours. Do not bow the knee to the *archas*, rise up in righteousness and wrestle with that thing. Put it down in Jesus' name.

Go to your child's room and pray. We will be with you in spirit. Call upon the Lord to show you the ploy of the *archas* and announce that Jesus was here first. He has claim to your family through your prayers. Go ahead, rejoice.

Yes, you do have the right to go into that room! You have every right to stand there and to proclaim the Power Presence of the Lord. You have every right to speak to that child in the name of Jesus! Yes, you do have the right to speak into his life, to bind those forces set against him. Take it on in the spirit. Do not back down! You do have the right to embrace that child.

The *exousias* would try to defeat you by telling you that you have no right to rejoice. *"Who do you think you are to come into this place and proclaim Jesus?"* is the thought this force uses when it realizes it has been found out. Go get it! Blast that thing in the name of Jesus. You have every blood-bought right to rejoice in the face of the Enemy. Sing the song of Jehoshaphat. Sing the song of Moses. Get that rejoicing going because you are driving the Enemy into the sea and it shall soon close over its head. Drive the devils out with the sound of praise!

The *ponerias* has been trying to bring destruction to your family through this type of rock music. Look at the videos, the posters, the styles. They destroy the people who make the music and the people who listen to it, but not yours. You are in the gap. The wolf has grabbed the wrong lamb this time. Through you your family and their friends will be delivered. Take it on in the Spirit.

The *ponerias* operates through terror. Call it what it is, a defeated foe. You are not going to believe the lie that your loved one will be involved in drugs and violence. You are going to think according to your prayers and relate to that person according to the Word of the Lord. Hear from God. Rehearse the promises over that bed and in that room. Anoint their CD's and tapes with oil and call upon the Lord to deliver them.

DEFEATING FEAR

There is no fear in Christ because perfect love casts out all fear. As a parent I know what it is like to see your child head for the world and have to be prayed back. As a teen ager, I rebelled against my godly parents. My mother prayed herself to sleep many nights as I wallowed in a drunken stupor. The longer my hair grew, the longer she prayed. She did not back down from my ugly words and deeds, but took on new determination in prayer.

My return to the Lord's ways took seven years. My mother never gave up. She interceded with great love often refraining from any correction. Her silence spoke more than any angry outburst. She did not wrestle with this flesh and blood, but she did a spiritual work a spiritual way. Many nights I could hear her singing herself to sleep with the hymns she knew so very well. At first it would make me very angry, as the *ponerias* raged through me, and then I would gain comfort in knowing that she loved me.

You can, through rejoicing in the face of the forces, deliver your entire home, office, or school from the devices of the Devil. You do not have to cringe in fear. You can rise up and proclaim the victory of Jesus, because all successful spiritual endeavor comes forth from an atmosphere of worship. Rejoice in the Lord always and again I say rejoice. His promise is greater than your problem!

Moses realized with the closing of the sea that Israel had been redeemed. He had cause to sing as the Lord had shown him the defeat of the horse and the rider. They were cast into the sea!

The song of Moses came from a heart encouraged with the fulfillment of a vision. Moses held God's promise that, as he entered in before the people and Pharaoh, God would move to set the people free. The cry of the people had come up before God and He was going to deliver the people from their hard bondage. Moses had to enter into the situation in order to work that deliverance.

ENTERING IN

Entering in is the action word of intercession. To step between a rebellious teen and his course of action isn't often pleasant. One father of five suggested to me the proper word picture for such an action is "velvet steel," that is, very soft to the touch, but very difficult to bend.

Moses had to face pressures from family, Pharaoh, and those he was trying to serve. Each one rejected him. The family rejected him because of the circumcision required by the covenant conditions (Exodus 4:25). Pharaoh rejected him because of the *archas* which had possessed him (Exodus 7:13). Until his royal highness became his broken lowness, Moses was an unwelcome visitor to Egypt. Even Israel rejected him because he called them to God (Exodus 20:19-21).

Moses still stood in that gap. He faced rejection as Christ would have, with a discipline of going to God. He found his fellowship in the One who had promised. He took solace in the One whose voice was as thunder and whose presence was as the spring rain. Moses became the friend of God, His prayer partner on the earth, the one on whom God could call for fellowship. He became the disciple of the true and living God.

He was a walking warrior. Each day he had to discipline himself to walk in the ways of God. Each day he heard the complaints of thousands who refused to enter into the promised rest. Each day he entered into that place between a rebellious people and a loving God, and when the sea closed and the horse and the rider breathed their last, a song began to flow forth from his spirit.

It was a song inspired by the Holy Spirit. A song of triumph. A song of joy. In it was the faith which had carried him in that space and as he sang his faith was renewed. The Lord who had been his strength had now become his victory. God had manifested His victorious power.

How our heart rejoices as we see prayer answered. How the joy floods our soul when that rebellious one starts to renew relationship. How the joy floods our soul when the prodigal returns. Strike up the band and prepare the feast, we are going to rejoice. I stand with you right now in faith for that one for whom you are praying. Yes, the

Lord will do all we need to see them restored. As surely as the horse and the rider were cast into the sea, He will deliver the one for whom you are praying.

Worship. Announce. Rejoice. The weapons of our warfare are not carnal, but mighty through God for the pulling down of strongholds (2 Corinthians 10:4).

When we **worship** we see the throne of God.

When we **announce** we initiate the enemies of our loved ones in to the understanding we have received from the throne.

And when we **rejoice** we govern the thoughts of our minds and bring captive every thought through the knowledge of Christ.

Yes, it is a war, but the advance intelligence report has been received...We win!

CHAPTER 14
A Fresh Word

We were in Cam Low, Vietnam, with a returned American Marine. During the war he had been stationed here, and had come back to resolve his personal conflicts. He and his wife had joined our team to prayer walk in areas of former conflict. We were the contact team for the Prayer Through the Window initiative for unreached peoples groups in the 10/40 Window.

As we were praying at what used to be the gate to a large base where he had been stationed, he began to flash back. This was the moment his wife and I had been waiting for. As his mind flashed back and forth from then to now and back to then again, his eyes took on a very strange and distant look. He could not get his bearings on time and location. Fear overtook him and he started saying, "Where is it? It should be right there. Where is it?" He was looking for the gate which had meant safety so many years before, and indeed it was not there. The pavement which had entered the gate was there, but the gate itself was long gone.

"You're right," his wife said. "Old things have passed away, all things are become new" (2 Corinthians 5:17). The Word reached down into his heart. His mind cleared and his eyes focused. "Your right, all things are become new!" he announced. A joyful laughter bubbled out of him, and he announced that scripture over and over again to the forces trying to oppress him. "Old things are passed away, all things are become new." That word was for him, and announcing it set him free.

But the story doesn't end there. We continued our journey for several days, visiting the place where he had been wounded and med-evacked. We stood at the first place where he encountered enemy fire. We walked the trails where he had led patrols, and in every place he said, "It has all changed, old things are passed away, all things have become new."

What we needed in that prayer walk was a fresh word from God. The Lord provided it, and it became the anchor for our souls. Throughout Hanoi, and in every other part of the country, we received friendly greetings because we had the positive attitude that it is the will of God that every man, woman, and child in Vietnam have the opportunity to receive Jesus as their Lord and Savior in our generation. We were no longer fighting a previous war, we were declaring His victory in a new one!

At this writing, we have heard reports from throughout the country of a sweeping revival which is reaching the mountain people as well as the city dwellers. It is changing the look of Vietnam as another extension of the lie of Moscow comes tumbling down.

THE ANNOUNCEMENT

Ephesians 3:10 says the Church will announce to principalities and powers the manifold wisdom of God. The Greek word *gnorizo* means "to initiate into knowledge" according to W. E. Vine[1]. This is the role of the church. To initiate *archas* and *exousias* into the knowledge of the manifold wisdom of God. What is that wisdom? It is that Jesus was before all things, created all things, and will be worshiped by all things. Those things can be in heaven, on the earth, or under the earth but it doesn't matter because Jesus is Lord in all arenas of existence.

You are then to go forth into all the earth and declare that Jesus is risen from the dead and has vanquished the Enemy and all his forces. As an Attack Lamb, you go to the five pressure points and you initiate the *archas, exousias, kosmokratos*, and *ponerias* into the understanding that they are defeated. The battle is won, you are the announcer, "Four Forces, we have a decision. The winner and still Champion is Jesus Christ. You are dismissed!"

All conclusive battles are won with praise and worship. Worship is a dialogue with God. It is the language of intimacy with the Holy Spirit which releases confidence in us, and an earthly agreement with Him. It is imperative for every Attack Lamb to maintain a worship discipline. This dialogue with Jesus is the heartbeat of Christian experience.

As we celebrate our salvation in a worship service, we praise Him. This is the sacrifice of praise. Then, when you park your ark on some totally corrupt corner and choose to praise the Lord, you initiate a dialogue. Speaking in the power of the Holy Spirit, you give witness to what you see. That witness is true because it cannot be contaminated by intellect and emotion.

Praise is what opened the prison door for Paul, and it will break the yoke of bondage on those around you. As you praise, you definitely serve notice to the *archas* and *exousias* that there is someone present who can speak mysteries to God. They are dreading the moment just as the demoniac in Mark 1 dreaded the arrival of Christ.

We must dialogue with Jesus about His will in a place. In the history of King David, he asked about every movement. He did not presume that yesterday's plan would bring today's victory. Instead, he sought the Lord for every move. We must also ask the Lord for perception. "What is going on in this place from Your point of view?" is our operative question.

He responds according to His promise, **"If any man lack wisdom, let Him ask of God who freely gives and does not upbraid."** (James 1:5 author's paraphrase). He shows us what combination of the four forces are at work in that place. As we wait on Him, He will give tremendous insight. Chinese leaders in many countries have expressed their amazement at the insight which I have been given concerning the clans and power structures in China. Only a Chinese should know these things. In discussions with Taoist believers, they have expressed amazement at the way the Lord has instructed us to pray. A Westerner should not know these things.

This perception has been gleaned as a result of hours of intercession in the five pressure points of these nations. God will show you as you seek Him. Ask the Lord to give you perception into the power structures of your community. Ask Him as you walk through the place where you live just how the four forces are preventing your loved ones from hearing the Gospel. Get the insight from Him.

PRAYING WITH GOD'S PERCEPTION

Next, we pray according to the perception the Lord gives us. I shall never forget sitting in the replica of Lenin's office and realizing the man had, with the help of the *archas*, persuaded nearly two-thirds of the world there was no God. When the Lord showed us that the lie was empowered by the four forces, it became defeatable. I did not have to defeat them again! Jesus has already won that battle! I just had to announce that there was one person in that place who knew Jesus Christ in a personal way. One word of truth defeated the power of the lie. This is *really* praying with the understanding.

Jesus will then give you the word to speak. He has promised if we will say what we hear from Him, and will do what He shows us to do, we cannot lose. We are not leaderless as we stand in that gap. We are in dialogue with the Commander. He has direct access to our spirit as we pray.

THE WORD FOR NOW

So many people make a list of "warfare scriptures" and at this point in their prayers begin reciting the long list. Now, I do believe the Word of God which He sends forth will not return void, but will accomplish that for which it is sent (Isaiah 55:11); but I also believe we are to hear from the Lord in every situation with a current word which He would have us speak.

In our work in Asia, there are many times when what opens the door of utterance to a monk or a temple leader is not a statement, but a question. I ask the Lord to bring to my mind the right question to lead this man a step closer to Christ. Understand, the sinner lives a hopeless existence whether they are part of a religion or just a free thinker. In either case they have no hope. The Lord gives me the questions, and they plumb the depths of their understanding of their own hopelessness. They invariably come to the conclusion that they need Jesus.

Try this, instead of presuming to speak to a situation, ask the Lord to give you the *rhema* word, the now word for the place.

Recently in Saigon a group of Attack Lambs related to me the story of a prayer walk which they had taken to a center of education, one of the five pressure points that change a nation. This was the center for preparation and administration of the youth movement of Vietnam, those red-scarfed young armies so visible in communist countries. The team had walked about the walled facility for several hours and then had taken up prayer watches on the four corners. The compound is about a block square with the dominant feature of an old temple in the center.

The team was praising God quietly and announcing the name of Jesus.

After half hour on location they were startled by a loud crashing sound. They opened their eyes to see that the old temple in the midst of the compound had just collapsed. The next day they read in the local paper about the collapse. There were no injuries and officials were completely without explanation for how it happened. There were no explosives in the area. **The temple had just collapsed!** The team is certain the Lord knocked it down as a sign that He is setting the children free. Now is the time for children's workers in Vietnam.

WHAT MUST I DO?

During the same visit the Attack Lambs met with leaders from across the country of Vietnam. I was told of the experience in a northern province where the prayer walking Attack Lambs had been at a center of government. They had praised, prayed, perceived, prayed according to the perception and were speaking the word of the Lord to the building saying, "Give up the souls of men!"

Then, from the building emerged a party leader. The Lambs were in twos and spread out so they could not be mistaken for any sort of political group. The man walked right up to one pair and asked, "What must I do to become a Christian?"

In spite of being startled and concerned about arrest, they responded, "You must repent, ask Jesus into your heart, be baptized and burn your party membership card." They were delighted to report he has done all these things, and is now being discipled in a small group. All over South East Asia the reports are the same. As teams implement the dialogue, God gives them souls.

A PROPHETIC ACT

Occasionally the Lord will lead you to a "prophetic act." This is some action which will result in a breakthrough for souls in a nation. Jesus says, "What you see me do, that do." Prophetic acts are representative demonstrations in the natural of something God is implementing in the realm of the Spirit.

I was in Brunei, taking a walk and praying. I was the guest of a member of Gideon's 300, and I was very excited to visit this small but significant country. In the course of our prayer walk, we became aware of the history of Islam on the island of Borneo.

It was explained to us that a couple had come to Borneo from Arabia. Entering the mouth of the Brunei River, they made their way upstream, past the very treacherous currents at the neck, and then to the small village of Jujugong where the Murud people live. The Murud are headhunters.

The man of the couple said to stay alive among these savages, his wife must say she was his sister. (Sound familiar?) It didn't work. The headman of the village, who was the third Sultan of Brunei, took the woman to be his wife. They conceived a son, the fourth Sultan, and when she was sure he was healthy and strong, the woman killed the third Sultan and threw him into the river.

The woman was a fierce leader, and the son followed her example. He declared Islam to be the faith of the Brunei people; hence, the situation as it is today.

We went to Jujugong and verified the location on the river where the Sultan's body had been thrown in. It is now marked by a site which is attended only by chickens and a few teens very interested in foreign guests. The Murud are no longer headhunters, and the current Murud headman verified that, indeed, this was the place, and we had the legend right. We prayed there and asked the Lord to remove the curse from the land and the people, and to open them to the good news of Jesus.

As we were praying with this perception, the Lord showed us we should take up the Brunei River by the tail as Moses picked up the serpent. Our location near the head waters of the heavily silt-laden stream was in fact the tail. As we stood on a jetty, one member of our team took the place of the lady, and a Murud pastor the place of the man. They led in prayers of repentance for Islam coming to the island.

Then we took a bottle of drinking water and, praying the Lord would remove the curse from the river, we poured it in. We sang and danced to the joy of the local teens and then went on our way. We shared the experience with several prayer warriors and I returned to Singapore.

Several months later, we wanted to hold a Prayer Walking Seminar in Brunei. Again, the Gideon's 300 member was volunteered to try to use his influence to make the arrangements. But to have an open meeting there would require an invitation from the Bishop of Kuching. This dear brother has the incredible responsibility of maintaining an open door for Christ in the middle of a Moslem nation. His faith is tremendous.

Weighing the decision, and thinking that people who dance about on jetties and pour water into rivers might be a bit extreme for the delicate balance he has to maintain, he was reported to be a little reluctant to endorse us to the Religious Affairs Bureau.

The time for decision had come and he committed it to much prayer. We too asked the Lord to do something which would confirm the Seminar. On the morning of the last day in which the decision could be reached, the Brunei Bulletin headline read, "Clear Water Phenomenon Occurs in the Brunei River." It just so happened that on that day, from a jetty at Jujugong to the mouth of the river, the water ran completely clear!

This was the first time anyone could remember such a thing happening. Children swam in the river and new species of mature fish were caught by fishermen. The Sultan invited specialists to come and examine the river to see what had, in fact, caused this to happen, but they were totally at a loss to explain it.

The invitation came and we had a wonderful seminar which was climaxed by a visit to the *istana* (palace) of the Sultan of Brunei. We also received his personal handshake and greeting! The Lord loves him. It is the will of God that the Sultan and his family enter into a personal relationship with Jesus and be saved and healed. Jesus loves the Sultan enough to change the nature of his river.

I tell you that as you go into the gaps of the world and announce to *archas* and *ezousia* the manifold wisdom of God, Jesus will change rivers to open doors for you.

THE REAL ACTION

Prophetic actions are a part of prayer walking, but the real action is in the dialogue. Through worship you have the ability and calling to walk with God on this earth and to participate with Him in His purpose of bringing the Gospel to every person. You can speak life where death has reigned. You can be a way of provision to people who have less than nothing. People, whose spiritual poverty makes their earthly poverty look like riches, become sufficient in both realms because the *kosmokrat*os had to flee the Lion in you.

In the course of this dialogue between you and Jesus, there comes a time when the Lord gives you a release in your spirit that the purpose of your prophesying has been accomplished. Some refer to it as a "release," others a "peace," some a "breakthrough." For me it is a secure knowing that Jesus has heard my prayer. Not unlike the resolution of a conflict in the home, this peace releases torrents of love. It is the product of intimate relationship. There is a vast difference between reading a scripture from a list and claiming something has been done, and actually praying until the release is manifest in your spirit, and then humbly proclaiming what the Lord has done.

You are an Attack Lamb. Jesus has sent you forth as a sheep among wolves. Those wolves are in big trouble. You go to those pressure points where the Dagons of today are and park the ark. Keep that dialogue going.

We praise Him and He opens our hearts to worship. We pray for perception and He gives us understanding. We pray according to that perception and He gives us the word or action for the time. We speak the word of the Lord in the anointing of the Spirit, and He gives the release. We proclaim the victory which is to come, and Jesus watches over His word to perform it.

THE KEY TO PRAYER

Thanksgiving is the key to prayer! There is nothing greater in life than to walk and talk with the Lord, to celebrate in His great joy, and to know the fellowship of His broken heart for the nations. To see the world from His point of view is a maturing thing. It allows no room for anger with man. It gives no place to the work of the Devil. It calls unrighteousness sin and sees millions under the pain of a hopeless existence.

Through dialogue with Jesus we enter into a selflessness which no longer claims the means to soothe the emotional, but cries for the reality of the Spirit through which the yoke is broken and the captive freed. You are called as was John to enter into that heavenly scene and to dialogue with Christ, to hear Him say, "Who will go for us?" Live your life in the impact of His powerful presence.

Go ahead, get in the action. Give yourself to it. Rivers will change, temples will crumble, your enemies will walk up to you and ask to be saved because you are in a dialogue with Jesus, and He never fails.

Announce it to your world! There is a God, He has a Son, His name is Jesus, I know Him personally and you can too.

CHAPTER 15

Dawn of a New Day

W
hile working in Repale, India, I witnessed the dawn of a new day for the people there. A young, American missionary had traveled from Nepal to where we were, and her journey had been extremely difficult. While working in the mountains of Nepal she had fallen and broken her leg so severely she had to be carried for several days just to get out of the mountains. An even longer trip brought her to Kathmandu for treatment. But during the time it had taken her to get there, the bones of her leg had begun to fuse incorrectly. Now her leg had to be rebroken and set properly.

By the time she arrived in India, she was acquainted anew with agony. But she had also tasted the love the Asians have for anyone who will suffer hardship to come to them. Her heart was filled with love for the Lord and the people.

We were scheduled to minister in an evening crusade and had stretched out at a friend's home to rest. This young lady sat in the room, her plaster-bound leg supporting the guitar, and she began to pick a tune and sing.

Before long she had shifted over into singing in an unknown tongue. I joined with her and with full heart we sang a song in a language we had never heard. There was a sweet melody and descant. The rhythm was as foreign as the words. Time stood still as our voices filled the air with this spiritual song.

My reverie was broken by a sound at the window. We could see a crowd of people standing outside. When I went to the window and looked out I saw the house was surrounded. Other people were running to the house. We had no idea what had happened until our host exclaimed, "They have heard you sing the praises of God in their own dialect. Never have they seen a white woman or man who could play their rhythms and sing their songs. They want to know how this is possible."

She remained in India for many months, and gained such a reputation for the healings which occurred while she sang, that she was "invited" by the government to leave.

To this day you can go among those villages and they will tell you of the lady with the plaster cast who praised God in their tongue, and after whom there followed great signs and wonders. It was truly the dawn of a new day for those people.

DISCIPLE A WHOLE NATION

In these last days before the return of the Lord, the Holy Spirit is moving us to the uttermost parts of the earth and giving us strategies to disciple a whole nation.

The Egyptians and the Israelites had an interesting relationship. The Israelites were intimidated by the Egyptians because they were in power. But the Egyptians were also intimidated by the Israelites because of their great numbers. The Israelites were left leaderless and isolated by this intimidation. They felt they had no right to speak. This prevented them from hearing the word of deliverance which Moses brought.

Moses won in warfare, but he had to overcome the Four Forces which had arrayed themselves in the gap between the children of Israel and God. The Hebrews had become slaves and were being used to build the temples of false gods, and had no recourse. In their fear of the Hebrews, the Egyptians had become malicious. Each step forward for Israel brought planned retribution from the courts of Pharaoh.

Moses had to walk in three disciplines to experience his success. If they were necessary for Moses, it would do us well to adopt them for our use as well. Just as he was sent to disciple a whole nation, you have been sent by God to your gap to win too.

In the next few chapters we will be talking about the disciplines necessary for spiritual warfare, how to define a nation through five pressure points, and four keys to reaching any people. Moses lived out these disciplines and stood in the gap for Israel, you too will win in warfare as you disciple a whole nation.

THE FIRST DISCIPLINE: WORSHIP

Paul writes to the Ephesian church,

> **And be not drunk with wine, wherein is excess; but be filled with the Spirit; speaking to yourselves in psalms and hymns and spiritual songs, singing and making melody in your heart to the Lord; giving thanks always for all things unto God and the Father in the name of our Lord Jesus Christ; submitting yourselves one to another in the fear of God.**
>
> **Ephesians 5:18-21**

Why are they encouraged to have a song in their hearts? Because the heart is desperately wicked (Jeremiah

17:9), and out of the abundance of the heart the mouth speaks (Matthew 12:34). And we are commanded to guard our heart because the issues of life flow from it (Proverbs 4:23). To be successful in spiritual endeavor our heart must maintain its focus on the throne of God. We must discipline ourselves to focus on the throne and worship with the elders, angels, and beasts while false gods bow down. The first of three disciplines necessary for spiritual warfare is the **Worship Discipline.**

Paul's admonition to worship begins with separation from the world's source of joy. **"...be not drunk with wine wherein is excess;..."**

Those for whom you pray are drunk with the spirit of this age. It is nothing less than the *kosmokratos* of Ephesians 6:12. Emboldened by the illusion of power it supplies, children of the age declare their invincibility, self determination, right to choose, and indomitable self-will. As this generation slides down the lust-greased slope of amoral narcissism, the song playing loudly in the background will be, "I did it my way."

Paul's admonition is to those of us who will stand in the gap, reconciling the drunken and deceived so they will no longer participate in the wine of this age.

* * *

The **first essential** to the worship discipline is **determination** to no longer walk as the Gentiles, but walk in the Holy Spirit.

Excess is the trademark of this age. Marketing has focused more on this generation than any other. It is not uncommon to see children wearing shoes that cost more than $100 US. In many Asian capitols debt is extremely high as young people spend their future on the look of the Now Generation. The *kosmokratos* is placing them under the bondage of the age, which is excess. Sultans have fleets of cars, President's wives have rooms full of shoes. One ruling Democratic family boasts about twenty percent of the nation's Gross National Product being diverted into their family businesses.

In every country homes are destroyed by spouses who determine one partner is not enough, they must have more. The drive for more is actually killing the planet as we suck the resources from its depths to feed our excesses. Excess has caused brother to kill brother and father to kill son. Excess causes women to defy all natural law and kill the life which God has designed them to birth. Men declare, "Women have the right to choose," as though that life did not start with the man.

In an age gone wild with excess, you enter the gap. You realize a man's life does not consist of the things which he possesses. You have to make a determined decision to walk a separate path. You must reject the song of the world in your heart, and be filled with the Holy Spirit.

As God fashioned the ark of the covenant, so He has fashioned you with one purpose, to bear His glory into the presence of the gods of this age and see them bow down before Him. Yours is a mighty calling from a mighty God.

* * *

The **second essential** to worship discipline is **disembarkation**. The world is on a ship headed to hell. They are surrounded by the sirens of the sin-sick sea which sing songs of sensuality. (Whew!) But **you** must get off the boat. There is no mid-point. No compromise will be acceptable if you are going to stand in the gap. The evangelist may be able to identify with the people. The contemporary musician may be able to develop a sound similar to that of the world, but you are an intercessor and you **must** disembark. Moses could not continue in the ways of Egypt. Just as Israel was going to spend forty years in the wilderness, he did first. He had to get Egypt out of his heart before he could lead the hearts of his people out of Egypt.

Through his worship discipline Moses found that the wine of the God's Spirit was preferable to the fine tastes of Egypt. The appetites which once caused him to sin were now closed to Pharaoh's temptation. Moses' passions now focused on God as he stood silently before the Four Forces. He was not intimidated, he was given God's right to speak, he could not be bought off, no weapon formed against him could prosper. The baby of the bulrushes was now the pilot of the ship of salvation charting the way of his nation through intercession.

* * *

"...be filled with the Spirit;...," Paul continues. Spiritual work must be done a spiritual way. This nineteenth verse of Ephesians 5 gives us the **third essential** to worship discipline. We must **declare** the worthiness of God.

For Moses to declare the worthiness of God to the people, he had to first have a revelation in his own spirit. He had seen the burning bush and stood on the holy ground. His hand had been made leprous and healed again. His staff had been brought to life. His thoughts spoken back to him. He had come to realize that the Lord is greater than anything created, because He was before all things. Moses could declare the power, presence, person, and purpose of God, because they had met and walked together in the mountain.

Paul admonishes the Ephesians and us to maintain that throne room power through the exercise of the tongue in different ways. First, we are to speak in psalms. Next, we are to speak in hymns. Third, we are to speak in spiritual songs.

What is common to all three? We are to speak. When you speak, the ear nearest to your mouth is your own ear. You believe what you say. When you testify to others, you are encouraged because you are hearing one of the ways in which we overcome the Accuser...with the word of our testimony (Revelation 12:11). You are listening as you talk.

The doors to the nations are open; God has opened them. You will either talk your way into them or you will tell yourself a million reasons why you are not going. You will determine what song you hear for you are the singer.

As an Attack Lamb, you control the environment around you. The song in the air will be the one you put there as you worship the Lord. How refreshing it is to hear a kind or polite word. How refreshing is a positive report. A good report from a far land is like a glass of cool water (Proverbs 25:25). You will bring refreshing to your soul and those around you as you sing the Psalms.

THE WINNING POWER OF WORSHIP

One time in Canton, China, I was sitting in the coffee house of a restaurant waiting to return to Hong Kong. Our group had been successful in delivering a large number of bibles to the church and we were rejoicing. As we sang, we spoke out in the song of the Holy Spirit, singing in a language we did not understand.

Adjacent to us was a table of students. In their twenties, they were very much into the new image of China. Their cigarette smoking was not as bad as their beer belching and loud shouting. As we sang they began to weep. One of them spoke to our leader, who did not understand what was said. The young man spoke again in Mandarin Chinese.

"How do these Westerners know our dialect?" he asked.

"They do not," replied our leader.

"Yes, they are singing about Jesus and His love for us, we want to confess our sins and receive Him as the song says." His tear-streaked face and remorsefully repentant voice confirmed his sincerity. The entire group opened their hearts to the Lord that afternoon.

Martin Luther declared the Spirit to be ours. Paul says to sing "spiritual songs." The Corinthians are encouraged to sing with the Spirit and with the understanding (1 Corinthians 14:15). While many songs are spirited and music is used in many cultures to invoke a certain spirit,

Paul is talking here about the song of the Holy Spirit birthed in our hearts.

Declaring Christ among the nations is the result of a **worship discipline**. As you practice His praise, you will see His glory. Speak in psalms, hymns, and spiritual songs making melody in your heart to the Lord.

By exercising our tongues in these three ways, we declare Christ's worth in the Word, in the history of the Church, and today. **The worship discipline is vital to spiritual warfare.**

The word of your testimony joins with that of the Church, and the Rock of Ages calls you to His ranks of Attack Lambs. You march with Judah in the army of Jehoshaphat and watch as the Moabite and Ammonite fall before you.

Judah declared the worthiness of God. Moses and David declared the worthiness of God. You, as a worshiping warrior, must declare the worthiness of God. Moab, Ammon, and Seir fell before Judah. Pharaoh fell before Moses. Goliath fell before David. The Dagons of today **will** bow down before you as you declare the worthiness of God.

The worship discipline develops a focus on the throne of God. As you enter into the gap, you will need to maintain this focus. As it was with Moses, you will hear the sounds of government leaders, you will hear the sounds of elders, you will hear the sounds of family members, but above all you will hear the questioning sound of your own doubts. Will God really hear your prayer and save your nation?

As Moses remained focused on the sound of God, you must allow the thunder of the sound of many waters to drown out the other sounds. Government will tell you that you have the right to speak but when you try to exercise that right, you find they do not support you in your cause. You must allow the certainty of the throne to drown out the uncertainty of man.

LEADERS WORSHIPING

The leaders of churches are the hardest working group of people I know. They have my utmost respect. I can recall carrying five titles as a staff pastor in a local church. When people would come to me with an idea for another area of ministry, I would feel overwhelmed. I am afraid I was not as supportive as I could have been. I thank God for the times they would patiently pray until my mind would finally clear and I could hear what they were saying.

You may encounter this type of difficulty mobilizing Attack Lambs in your church. Please pray for those who are your pastors and leaders that they will also hear very clearly and focus on the throne of God.

Each time I inform my family members of travel plans, I know, while they support the work I am doing, they would rather I remain at home. Just as Moses' wife had to make major adjustments to the idea of covenant relationship and going down to Egypt, our families may have to adjust to the call on our lives.

Many fine Women's Aglow officers have had to walk this tight rope of submission. They have had to maintain their focus on heaven's throne and speak its peace to the throne of their home. The joy of worship has paved the way for them.

Worry wars against worship. "O what peace we often forfeit, O what needless pain we bear, all because we do not carry everything to God in prayer,[1]" the old hymn says.   As an "A" type self-motivator, I can easily fail in the worship discipline and begin to worry about management decisions in the Kingdom. I have to remember, **I'm not in management...I'm in sales**. The worship discipline begins with a sacrifice of praise, and I am not always adept at giving it. I am asking the Lord to make me faster with the worship, and eliminate the worry.

Moses maintained his focus on the throne of God. The voice of Pharaoh was silenced. The voice of the elders of Israel received a new song of thanks to our God. Moses' sister took up the tambourine and danced before the Lord, and Moses' own doubts were stilled as the Red Sea closed. The worshiping warrior had learned the delivering power of the discipline of worship.

Moses' dialogue with God teaches us an Attack Lamb strategy. You will one day stand before important people, seeking the freedom to declare Christ in your schools, towns, and places of business. Just as Moses did, you will need to hear the voice of God in the midst of the pressure of the gap. Just as Moses did, you need to practice a conversational relationship with God.

THE FOUR VOICES IN WORSHIP

The first voice in the dialogue with God is your **praise**. You offer it. It is birthed in your desire to proclaim Jesus as Lord of your life. We bring the sacrifice of praise in the face of opposition. Praise causes you to focus on the throne in the face of the Four Forces.

The second voice in the dialogue is the release to **worship**. This is different from praise. Worship is initiated in your spirit by the Holy Spirit. It is the inclusion of the Attack Lamb in the timing and anthem of heavenly expression. True worship is occurring as you allow the Holy Spirit to set you free from the preoccupation caused by the presence of the Four Forces. You are giving all trust to the Lord as you worship.

Flowing with the Spirit, you begin to declare the worth of God. This is initiated in your spirit as the depth of devotion divulges the desire of the born-again heart. This draws open the curtains of intimacy with Christ. This worship invites His participation in further dialogue.

The third voice is that of **blessing**. He will speak a promise to your heart. In corporate worship, the gifts of the Spirit will manifest. Jesus is blessing the believer or congregation with an answer to their needs. Because He is manifest both in corporate and private devotion, we must develop the discipline of worship to release the blessings He has for us.

The fourth and final voice is returning **thanks** to Him, which is a form of praise. The conversation is complete as we return thanks, and the process begins again. When we have this dialogue as a discipline incorporated in our daily experience, we begin to hear the heart of God for our family, our church, our city or our school. The discipline of worship is God's school to teach you His voice.

He speaks today, as always, to give direction to the deliverers of this age. Those who are His children hear His voice, and enter into dialogue with Him for the benefit of the nations.

CHAPTER 16
The Word of Light

The second discipline necessary for spiritual warfare is the **Word Discipline**. It is through the soul-saving, incorruptible seed of the Word that we gain a place of ministry and the ability to perform it. By the strength and light derived from this discipline, we have the power: to dispel darkness from the peoples of the earth, to establish the government of God in all we do, to exercise the ministry gifts God has bestowed, and to manifest His Power Presence.

God said, "Light be," and light dispelled the darkness. We used to play a little game with our children who were afraid of the dark. We would turn on a light and try to find where the darkness would hide, because the darkness is afraid of the light. Together with the child we would look under the bed, but when we shone the light under there, there was no darkness. We would look in the closet, but when we opened the door, we could find no darkness for the light had dispelled the darkness. When we looked deep into the toe of the last pair of discarded shoes deep in the corner of the closet, we could see a little darkness, but that was certainly not enough to keep us awake, and we certainly would not be afraid of something hidden that deep in the toe of an old shoe. In fact, if we threw out the shoe, we could throw out the darkness at the same time.

While this is a child's game, it has truth for us. The darkness is strong only until some Attack Lamb starts to shed light on it. The light will dispel the darkness.

When Jesus asked, **"Will you also leave me?"** Peter replied, **"Lord, to whom shall we go, you alone have the words of eternal life"** (John 6:68 author's paraphrase). Attention Attack Lambs: to bring nation-changing revival, we must first study to show ourselves approved unto God. Until we are disciplined in the Word, God will not entrust the lives of those for whom He died to you.

NO ONE IS HOME

So often I look into the eyes of those around me when I travel to foreign countries, only to realize there is no light in the soul I am seeing. Often I comment, "There is no one home." The real shock comes when the person is someone I think highly of. Until they know Christ, the light will not shine forth from those eyes. It is my daily prayer that the darkness will be dispelled and light will fill the void.

In the Genesis account of creation we find that darkness covered the face of the deep. And then..."God said." God spoke to the darkness. Man, is that ever a power principle! God spoke, David spoke, Moses was supposed to speak, Jesus said...speak to the mountain.... We are really onto something here!

God said, "Light be," and there was. Isn't this what we want to see happen to those around us? Isn't this the cry of your heart, you who have entered into the gap to intercede to reconcile man to God? Isn't this what you want to see for your parents and children?

WHEN THE LIGHT COMES ON

Can you imagine the light coming on in your school or place of work? Just think how it would be if this afternoon the light of the Gospel came on in the minds in Jakarta or Beijing. Imagine the light coming on in the United Nations when they realize only Jesus can bring true peace to the world. Imagine OPEC when the light comes on!

It works the same way in our lives, beloved. As we exercise our Word discipline, we dispel the darkness in our lives.

Often I'm asked where a person should go to prepare for ministry. I tell them the first place to go is to their own Bible, and study. When they assure me they are ready to launch out, I gently ask them to name the books of the Bible. Then I ask for the theme, time, and setting of each book. By then the would-be Attack Lamb realizes what I am saying. The Word discipline must be established for the darkness to be dispelled.

ATTACK LAMB LIFESTYLE

So many Christians have a sense of salvation but little, if any, idea of the Attack Lamb lifestyle. They are always asking directional questions. They have no lamp for their feet. They certainly are not equipped for spiritual warfare because they lack discipline.

Matthew 10 teaches the lifestyle of the Attack Lamb. It is this lifestyle which separates the disciple from the believer. In the Sermon on the Mount, Jesus indicates the impact those who walk in the power of His Word are going to make on the community and the globe. Darkness is dispelled from their minds as He teaches them how to relate to Him and to each other, and to the world around them. He is very clear they must love each other, as well as those whom they hope to reach.

In like fashion, He instructs the disciples they are not to be encumbered with the cares of this life as they go out to those who are in those fields ripe unto harvest. They are to bring healing and deliverance and proclaim the Kingdom of God. The government of all affairs is to be seen in the light of the Gospel.

YOU—A LIGHTHOUSE

When you enter into the gap and face the Four Forces, they are dispelled by the light of truth. You have become the "lighthouse" to direct your friends and neighbors away from the rocky shores of this age and into the safe harbor of Christ's love.

Imagine how the shadow of **intimidation**, the first force, must flee when the light of the perfect love which casts out all fear shines from your eyes. You are not afraid of the terror by night or the destruction at noon day (Psalm 91). The love that Jesus has placed in your heart allows you the freedom to dispel the darkness from your environment. You have become the indomitable force upon whom the threats of ungodly Goliaths have no effect.

The **right to speak** is the second force you can now dispel from the security of your "lighthouse." As you enter into the space between your community and Christ there will be forces who will say, "You cannot talk about Jesus here."

They will threaten to sue you. They will challenge the legality of your personal witness for Christ. They will try to cause you to lay down your God-given commission to name the name of Jesus. The light of the Word in your "Lighthouse" will drive them off.

I recently produced a TV special on "Christ in the Public Schools." The ACLU responded by threatening the school board of that community with lawsuit. Thank God for a principal and superintendent who responded with the light of the Gospel saying, "Do not threaten us. If you are going to court, go; but, be prepared for the battle of your life." The ACLU blinked first and backed away from the battle.

THE FEARLESS FIGHT OF LOVE

The third force you will dispel is that of **using people to get things**. As you demonstrate the love of Jesus through acts of kindness you dispel this power. The Lord, finding you interceding in the gap, will allow you to become aware of information. He will speak to you facts about those in the area so you can pray for them. As you pray for them, you will feel the love of Jesus beginning to flow out from you. His glorious Power Presence will accompany you to activities in the community, and those you have been praying for will be drawn to you.

Remember, they are used to being used. They will have their guard up and defenses at the ready. Be gentle. A kind word is often appreciated. You will notice that as you bring a cheerful greeting, a kind gesture, or a warm handshake, the *kosmokratos* will be dispelled. I have seen it time and again.

The counterattack will be the invitation to use your freedom in some kind of community action which uses people for their money or influence. Be careful. Do not take up the idols of the land. Let the governing principle of the Lord's provision keep you from opening the door of your Lighthouse to the *kosmokratos*.

The fourth force which the light shining from the windows of your eyes will dispel is **malice**. When Jesus looked into the eyes of the rich young ruler, the man began to be drawn to the government of God. When Jesus looked into the eyes of the woman taken in adultery, she too was drawn to the government of God, finding it far more gracious than man's. So it is with those around you. As you pray for them, there will be a time when their eyes will meet yours and malice will flee.

167

There is so much talk of racial division in our age. "Ethnic cleansing" has become the phase replacing "genocide." In the modern-speak of our one-world-government age, malice is justified by family planning and overpopulation. Genocide in Europe and Africa now spreads into the Western world as hate-crimes increase. Governments trade in horrible alterations of God's creation so that the wonder of atomic structure and genetic order now becomes demons of agonizing destruction, and the systems to deliver them are big business among the nations.

THE POWER OF ONE

Who are you in the face of such global power? Once while sitting in the gap for the Soviet Union, I had the most wonderful experience. I was in the replica of Lenin's office in Moscow. Our prayer team had been walking and praying in that city for several days. It was the Spring of 1985.

The tour group had passed on but, with permission from the guards, I remained to contemplate the overthrow of Communism. How was this manifestation of malice to be removed from the earth? Two-thirds of the globe was at that time under the forces emanating from that place. As an intercessor, I had entered into the gap to hear the Word of deliverance from the Lord.

The Lord quickened to me that communism was just the horse. The rider was atheism. Marx, in rebellion to his Jewish parents, had never addressed the subject of faith. Into this void the State had entered so young people were trained to call on Lenin for provision. Our team had a very meaningful encounter with Jews in Siberia on our way to Moscow from Beijing and the thoughts of Stalin, the ethnic cleanser of his age, were still very fresh in my mind. He had determined to wipe out faith in a generation.

As I sat there praying, I asked the Lord for insight. "What will dispel the darkness of the lie of atheism?"

I was startled with the speed and clarity of His response, "One word of truth."

That was it. I left the Lenin museum and crossed Red Square to the famous bell tower gate of the Kremlin. There the tower clock set the pace for several hours of prayer walking. I walked around that bastion of atheism declaring, "There is a God, He has a Son, His name is Jesus, He died for me."

As I walked and prayed, I had the distinct sense that the fountain of atheism was being sealed by the Rock of Ages. I tell you, it was a marvelous feeling to know that the *pneuma tae ponerias*, the spirit of malice, was being dispelled from millions under the repression of communism. I felt that, for my purposes, the axe was laid to the root that day.

Not too many years later the entire enterprise of the USSR came to a screeching halt. For me and the many teams we accompanied and sent into the Soviet Union, as well as the millions of intercessors around the world, the day the Berlin wall came down was one of the sweetest victories ever. Intercession is the key to release for millions in darkness today.

A SPECIAL MINISTRY?

Is this a "special ministry?" Are those who walk the earth in prayer called with a "unique calling?" No! In recent years the prayer movement has grown larger than any one organization. Even with the wonder of the Internet and global communication capabilities, the answers to prayer are happening so rapidly they will be recorded only in heaven's throne room.

I have noticed a common thread in those whom the Lord is using in this great time of prayer. They all demonstrate three characteristics.

First, they are all **filled with the Word of God**. Their conversation is the Word. They encourage each other from the Word. What they do not do is sit around and tell war stories and demonstrate the arrogant one-up-manship of previous groups. These prefer to remain irrelevant, giving all glory to the Lord.

Second, they are **humble**. They realize their identity is hidden in God and He has given them their area of responsibility. Their attitude is one of being in awe of His grace at even having been included. This humility is the foundation stone of their ministry. Most intercessors only become famous after their death. The purity of selflessness is thus maintained. Man may never know you have invested a lifetime of prayer for your city. But, heaven knows.

Third, they are **avid students of the Word**. God measures our lives by His own standards. Second Timothy 2:15 is the common doorway through which those working in the various continents have come, **"study to [show] yourself approved unto God."** There is no short cut to ministry.

Much study is indeed an aggravation to the flesh. The thought that after years of service the Lord could be calling you away from the business of the church to seek His face and study so He might prepare you to be with Him in the gaps of the globe is so radical very few enter in.

IT'S THE WORD

Developing the discipline to dig in the golden veins of God's Word is as difficult as becoming a brain surgeon. But to whom will that surgeon turn when he has done all he can if not that one whom the Lord has led into the situation? Standing by bedsides I have learned the Word of God takes precedence over all the instruction man can have. Faith is paramount. How does one prepare for the life-walk of holiness that is God's pathway to power?

Study the Word!

As I participated with a great team in birthing the Unreached Peoples movement, I often wondered why the

Lord had not entrusted these peoples to us before this. An interesting question was, why now? Why us? Why Dr. Barret? Why Dr. Winters? Why Peter Wagner? Why Dr. Foltz? Why Eric Watt?

One day George Otis Jr. left my home with manuscript in hand and I wondered, *"Why not his father?"* As I sat and watched Dick Eastman carry people from the couch of complacency to world-changing intercession, I wondered, *"Why such a mild mannered gentleman as he?"*

One morning in 1984 I was scheduled to speak at Christ for the Nations in Dallas. I arrived early and was so fortunate to hear Dr. Jonathan Chao deliver an update on the need for prayer for China. Then I spoke concerning teams for Nepal.

The next speaker was Loren Cunningham, so I waited to hear him. He spoke of the need for mobile ministry teams to cover the earth. Little did I know I would stand with him at the southern most point of the Asian continent eight years later and ask the Lord's forgiveness on behalf of all missionaries for the colonial attitude we have had toward the native populations, the "locals."

COMMON DENOMINATORS

As I continued to observe these men, several common denominators shown through. Humility and holiness were the first two; the third is they are all men of the Word. Each one is governed by the Word in his heart. Each is a man of discipline. Each is a man of prayer. Each keeps his emotions governed by the Word. Each has prioritized his life to be found where God wants him, and to be doing what God wants him to do. And, finally, each is willing to wait for an eternal reward.

Two particular meetings with Dick Eastman have affirmed and illustrated the value of keeping the Word in one's heart.

We met at the train station in Canton, China. He

was so excited because he had been able to bring some Bibles into the country without being detected. Then, I watched as his first act in this success was to pause and give thanks to the Lord. An act of humility from someone whose emotions were being governed by the Word in his heart.

The second meeting was in Warsaw, Poland, the week after the Chernobyl nuclear incident. He was aware of the cloud of radioactivity that shrouded the city of Warsaw that week. But he flew into that cloud anyway, just to keep an appointment with me which he believed God had ordained. As a result, the Change the World School of Prayer was translated into Polish and became a guiding light for prayer for the Catholic youth who wanted desperately to dispel the darkness of communist atheism from their land.

The common denominator of those involved in the global prayer movement is the deep treasure of the Word in their hearts. They live it out among the nations. They demonstrate its wisdom as they fill global gaps and pray. They are entrusted with ministry for they have studied to show themselves approved unto God.

These men have some common experiences. Each has taken a stand for the ministry to which they have been called. They have not always had the approval of man upon the directions they have chosen to go. While they have sought to be at peace with all, there have been times when God's approval has caused them to take a step beyond their peer group, and in so doing, have redefined leadership.

I shall never forget John Dawson preparing to write the great book, *Taking Our Cities for God* (Creation House). We were at a board meeting in Kansas City when John asked our pardon from meetings that year. He explained that he was going to be out of circulation for a year because the Lord was calling him to write. Here was a young man at the helm of a world-changing ministry, who was going to draw aside to the Lord and write. That book would become a tool of mobilization through which millions would come to Christ. Because of the Word discipline in his life, he was free to make such a decision and walk it through to fruition.

Because he spent time in the Word, the apostle John was able to define the practical directions necessary to dispel the darkness from a population center, Ephesus. We too can move in nation-changing effectiveness, when we have a Word discipline in our lives. God governs His actions through His Word. When we do the same, govern our actions by His Word, we bring ourselves into alignment with His purposes. Then we will have the wisdom to know when, where, and what to do, as He directs.

PRACTICAL SUGGESTIONS

Here are a few practical suggestions which will help you develop your Word discipline. First, select a Bible of a size, weight, feel, and typestyle that is as comfortable to you as though you had owned it all your life. It seems strange, but my Bible has a certain feel to it I really like very much. Like a gunfighter's Peacemaker in the Old West, your Bible has to feel "just right." I learned this from watching two men as they handled their Bibles.

Dr. Lester Sumral would take up his Bible to teach and heft it in his hand. He had a certain way of holding it; you just knew it was his Bible. It rested in his hand as a trusted friend, a constant companion.

When Dr. Costa Dier would open his Bible to teach, some of the pages were so worn you could no longer read the text. As he taught 75 points of leadership, those following were unaware he was not reading from the text. He had read those pages so much the ink had worn off them. That is a Word discipline.

Next, find a tool that will lead you through the Bible over a prescribed time period. Many intercessors I know, including myself, use the *Youth With a Mission Personal Prayer Diary* (Youth With A Mission Publishing). It combines Old and New Testament readings with some really good material on the nations. It's been my faithful Word companion for years.

Many pastors have found strength in their church reading through the Bible in a year. As the people develop their Word discipline, they move in common faith, which keeps the light on in the house and heresy out on the corner.

One of the things I do to keep current in the Word is to read the chapter of Proverbs that corresponds with the date. There are thirty-one chapters so most months it fits. I also multiply the date by five and read those chapters of Psalms so in a month the 150 Psalms become a part of the light in my house.

Pastor Peter Raphgi, a Tibetan, taught me to read a text and then ponder it by asking myself these questions:

What does this text tell me about God?

What does it tell me about unregenerate man?

What does it tell me about regenerate man?

What does it tell me about me?

Peter found the Lord while still a Buddhist monk. He had been under a vow of silence for seven years when one day the Lord appeared to him and led him through the Himalayas to Kathmandu, Nepal. There he heard the Gospel and was saved. He excitedly shared his deep joy that he could now speak and study the Word of God daily.

The Lord wants to speak to you through His Word. He wants to daily affirm His great love for you. As you prayerfully take up His Word, you demonstrate your love and respect for Him. It is to those who are faithful in the Word they have, that He will entrust the ministry which they do not have. This is the relational testing ground for the Attack Lamb. The Word discipline is essential to spiritual warfare.

CHAPTER 17

In Other Words...Work!

Jesus selected net menders as disciples. These fishermen were hardworking people who fed their families
from the labor of their hands. They fished at night,
cleaned and repaired their nets in the early morning
and spent the heat of the day resting. In this way they
made a living for their family. The nets were vital to their
existence, and more care and meticulous time was spent
on them than on the fishing itself.

The work of repairing the nets required great discipline. Each knot had to be inspected and tested. In case
of a frayed end or a tear, the damaged parts had to be cut
away and new fibers tied in its place. Undisciplined work
could mean hunger for that man's family, and perhaps the
entire village.

The Body of Christ is also a net, a global network of
cooperation to harvest that most precious of riches, the
souls of men. You are reading this book to become
equipped to fill one of the spaces in that network of intercession. As that net grows, and we become more skilled
in using it, people are coming to Christ in unprecedented

numbers. Don't be surprised to find yourself being knit together with believers you don't know in an ever-growing net of prayer.

Those who have studied and shown themselves approved unto God become "workmen." As intercessors, our work is clearly defined: we are to "enter in" between two with a view toward reconciling their differences.

THE THIRD DISCIPLINE...WORK

To be successful in this we must develop our **Work Discipline**, and add it to the disciplines of worship and the Word. Nowhere in Scripture is the importance of work and reconciliation and restoration more clear than Galations 6. Here Paul clearly defines several aspects of the work of reconciliation both for believers as well as in reaching the lost.

> **Brethren, if a man be overtaken in a fault, ye which are spiritual, restore such a one in the spirit of meekness; considering thyself, lest thou also be tempted. Bear ye one another's burdens, and so fulfil the law of Christ. For if a man think himself to be something, when he is nothing, he deceiveth himself. But let every man prove his own work, and then shall he have rejoicing in himself alone, and not in another. For every man shall bear his own burden.**
>
> **Galatians 6:1-5**

This apostolic instruction describes the fruit of the work discipline.

MENDING YOUR NETS

Jesus is still calling net menders. Here's how it works. The other day I took my son to the orthodontist. He is in the last stages of completing that American teenage ritual of braces to straighten his teeth. The patient following my son was a young girl who was also accompanied by her father. Now the doctor is a wonderful man and a real **net**worker. He introduced the girl's father and me to each other as "religious men." That term always makes me nervous because I never know what to expect. But in this case I was glad to find my new friend was a pastor and a prayer walker. We even found out we had prayed in the same places on different days.

Now he and I have a decision to make. Are we going to make the effort to keep in touch with each other? Are we going to do whatever is necessary to set aside the time to get together and to pray? It is going to require work to use this divine appointment to catch the "fish" who live in our common waters. Each of us is a new section of net for the other, one that has to be carefully woven in.

So it is with each of us. We can either put forth the effort to mend nets, or let them rot through neglect. The fibers the Lord uses to create, mend, and clean His nets are believers. But some of us suffer from being too busy to make these connections or keep them in good repair by speaking the Word, with its cleansing power, to each other.

It's easy to say, "Well, there aren't any fish to catch anyway." That's sour grapes. That person is a net destroyer. He is interested in something other than catching fish. Most of the time he is looking for personal recognition or another notch on his spiritual gun. His next move is to insist on fishing alone rather than surrendering his individuality to become a part of the net mender's team.

THE APPEARANCE OF IRRELEVANCE

The most effective intercessors are those who are content to appear irrelevant or extraneous to the situation for which they pray. The great labor for intercessors is to maintain this humble approach to their role of apparent irrelevance. This attitude walks hand-in-hand in unity with other workers in God's kingdom. The objective of the intercessor is reconciliation and restoration. They want those who are frayed or torn restored to the net and tied once again to the whole.

ON A LARGER SCALE

The power of unity in the Spirit was demonstrated to me during the Russian occupation of Poland in 1985. I was walking in a section of the old city. Unknown to me, the Lord had shown my face to people with the Light and Life movement of the Catholic charismatic youth in a vision several days before. They were astounded when they actually saw me. We had a divine appointment! As a result, I was invited to return to Poland and teach on the Person and Ministry of the Holy Spirit. I was thrilled at the way the Lord had brought us together.

Later, I shared this experience with some believers in the evangelical camp. Their response was less then enthusiastic. The hole in the net was gaping. They would not join together to mend this part of the net. I was still feeling quite overwhelmed that anyone in Poland had seen me in a vision. With such a clear mandate from the Lord to proceed, I was sure they would be eager to help. I asked the Lord for wisdom.

A charismatic priest I knew, Michael Sylvangia, had served with me as an occasional host of a nighttime TV show on Cornerstone Television in Pittsburgh. We got along quite well. We respected each other and accentuated the positives through fellowship on the common ground of Christ. At the Lord's leading I asked him to go with me on the teaching trip.

The Poles were thrilled; unfortunately, some of the Americans were not. Solidarity was the key word in Poland. They could see their oppressor very clearly. He lived in their neighborhoods and dominated their affairs. He was an uninvited guest in their villages, an unseen presence at every meeting. He operated through intimidation. He restricted their right to speak. He controlled their economy and his malicious acts had resulted in the martyrdom of their leader. The opponent to the faith did not have to be imagined, he was very real.

Mike and I were blessed to spend three weeks preaching and teaching among these wonderful people. It was an exercise in the work discipline. The shadow of Chernobyl clouded every meeting. Little did we realize that the Lord was causing the Soviets to be honest for the first time in the Cold War period. The veil had been rent. By standing side by side in Christ, Mike and I were a picture of the future of Poland.

Now don't get me wrong. At every turn there were opportunities to differ. We could have filled our time with doctrinal debates. Or we could have competed for the attention of the people. Or we could have entered into striving on anything from meals to speaking order. But we worked at unity. We worked at meekness. We worked at keeping our part of the net together. And we caught fish.

THE CONSUMMATE EXPERIENCE

The consummate experience was an invitation to the south of Poland to participate in a large youth gathering. Twenty-five thousand young people were coming to the home church of the Pope to celebrate the outpouring of the Holy Spirit, and we were invited to attend. Mike sat with all the priests and I was given the great honor of being with the dignitaries. The Bishop asked if he could serve me communion as a sign to these youth and a testimony to Poland that indeed their country had not been abandoned by the pentecostals and evangelicals of the West.

I was thrilled to help restore the breach. Today in Poland we are all enjoying the fruits of the post-cold-war era. Souls are being saved across that great land. One of the reasons was the work done by a few key people in restoring solidarity in the Body of Christ.

NET MENDERS BRING ACCEPTANCE

Of the many things Dick Eastman has imparted into my life, nothing is more meaningful to me than the phase, "He is accepted in over one hundred denominations." That takes a lot of work. It requires discipline not to offend. It also requires the wisdom of the Word to drive off the divisive forces of the Enemy and hold that net together for the sake of those who will be saved.

Did you catch that? **For the sake of those who will be saved.** How important is that? The words of the writer of Hebrews give us insight into how Jesus felt about it. **"Looking unto Jesus the author and finisher of our faith; who for the joy that was set before him endured the cross, despising the shame,..."** (Hebrews 12:2).

To succeed one must see beyond the immediate tensions of circumstances to the greater harvest to be accomplished if, in the spirit of meekness, we embrace each other across that net and hold on tight while the harvest is reaped.

THE FOURTH CONGRESS

When the Fourth Congress on Intercession in Indonesia was convened, I was asked to address the delegates. There were 250 delegates from every mainline denomination and many of the smaller independents. These meetings occurred just a week after many had been killed in political riots in the streets of Jakarta and everyone was concerned for the future of the nation.

As I rose to speak, I could feel the Holy Spirit stirring my heart with a word for these men. I am dwarfed in ministry by their incredible success as soul winners in the face of Islamic opposition. Their educations make me an intellectual pauper. Their testimonies could fill the earth. I was as meek as I have ever been.

"Men," I spoke with tremendous restraint, "our lives will not be measured by what we could have done with what we might have had. As we go forth from this point our lives will be measured by what we did with what we do have." As they cheered, I thought, *"Great, what comes next?"*

Through me, the Lord gave a great appeal for unity and for loving one another. It takes discipline to look into the face of one who has hurt you and continue to love. It takes tremendous discipline to release the offender into the hands of the Lord. So many times we allow the differences between us to pull the net apart. When we allow that to happen, the fish in the net slip away. And our life, and life's work, slips away with them.

THE CRISIS

America's teens are in crisis. The highest suicide rate is among teens. The number one cause of death among African-American youth is homicide. There is an epidemic of death in America. Why? Because the spirit of meekness through which the net could be mended has been replaced by the spirit of malice that wants to destroy the generation who can reach the globe with the Gospel.

It takes work to stand in that gap and call on God.

It takes work to walk those streets and pray. It takes work to enter that high school and pray. It takes work to rise before dawn and seek the face of Jesus to discover His ways of opening the doors to this generation.

For the American church, whose greatest labor of love is to make it to one Sunday morning church service each week, the challenge of reaching this teenage generation is overwhelming. Divorce in the Church has ripped families apart. The Church has become so much like the world that kids wonder why they should bother.

I was recently back in Singapore and noticed a young executive, who had really been growing in Jesus, wasn't there. His pastor explained to me the young man had seen the testimony of his mother compromised so many times he had come to the conclusion the whole thing was a game.

Each time a leader throws off the spirit of meekness and takes on an "I am somebody" attitude, the net gets another hole. Paul cautions us to be mindful of ourselves as we seek to restore another. In the ministry of restoration, we are kept by one thing: our work discipline. **The person doing the work the Lord has given them to do does not have time to be critical of the work of another.**

OUT IN THE FIELD

Over the twenty years I have spent taking short-term teams to the prayer points of the world, I have been blessed to build close relationships with many wonderful men and women of God, career missionaries. These tireless saints give their love and lives with remarkable dignity. They open their hearts and homes to many adventure seekers giving short-term missions a try for the first time.

Part of the briefing I give each team is the admonition to refrain from correcting the career missionary. For some reason those who go once in their busy lives feel they have the liberty to correct those who have given all.

I've seen this same phenomena occur when I've been a guest speaker. Once, on the ride from the airport to the church, I was urged to address a particular issue challenging the Senior Pastor of the church where I was going to minister. Imagine that, me presuming to address the life of a person who hourly stands in the gap for his flock. I don't think so. Even elders, who should know better, have asked me to mention things to pastors...as if I am the type of fellow who would hurt those who serve God.

While serving on the staff of several fine churches, I have had all the work I could handle just completing my own job description. I have no idea how others are able to do theirs.

After a few years of this you learn to discern those who have a good work discipline and those who do not. The conversation of those who are not working is death. They speak judgment and criticism and bring division. We are to speak healing into the Body of Christ.

So often I hear comments about the church. The worship could be more of this or less of that. Pastor could use a makeover, and did you see his wife's hair? The deacons lack discernment, and the youth minister is too radical. I wonder what all the negative talk is about. Imagine if the Lord heard what some think of His Body. Maybe His response would be, "Kind of pudgy around the wallet..."

ABOUT THE FATHER'S WORK

We are to be about the work of demonstrating the Father's love to each other and the world. This is the reason we stand in the gap, to reestablish the presence of His love in situations and among people where His love is no longer evident. We are to be Attack Lambs who manifest the glory of God as we pray for reconciliation.

My wife and I recently located our family in a community with seven churches among nine thousand people. Immediately there were rumors that we wanted to start the eighth church.

Actually, the Lord brought us there to pray for the churches. My wife Ellie and a friend have prayer walked each church. They have spoken the Lord's blessing, and Jesus has given them very specific instruction on prayer for each congregation. When I return from a trip to Asia, we always have a time of sharing concerning the local churches. We believe that Jesus sees one Church in the community and that Church meets in many buildings.

We feel that it is our role as Attack Lambs to stand in the gap and pray for the pastors. We pray that the Word of the Lord comes **to them** and forth **from them**. We ask the Lord to trim the wick of the church so the light of the Gospel burns brighter **through them**. We stand against any device of the Enemy set **against them**. This means we wrestle with the four spiritual forces set against their ministry.

One evangelical congregation in town announced a Saturday night praise and prayer meeting. They have never been known much for praise and prayer, so we count that a victory. The Pentecostal work in town is new. It has grown from 50 to 400 in just a few years. They have added a second Sunday service and are looking to Saturdays as well.

The young people in the Catholic church have begun reading the Bible, and are talking about being "born-again." Imagine that. They responded to "See You at the Pole," the annual youth prayer time for the schools. And a Bible club has begun in the local high school.

The principal of the elementary school retired. The new principal is an ordained Christian minister who is actively pastoring a church in another town and overseeing several Bible studies in neighboring communities.

CHANGE IS COMING

As we pray, we begin to see the lives of those in the community turn to the Lord. In each arena we could find reason for division and dissension. We could respond to the attempts of the Enemy to destroy the net that is gathering souls. We could fall prey to attacking individuals. It is work to stay out of divisive conversation which so fills the air of small towns. But we realize we are here to labor in the work of the Lord, not to divide.

Look around the church you attend. List ten things that are wonderful. When people find fault with the ministry ask them if they are praying about the perceived problem. If they say they are, then ask them why they are murmuring rather than standing in faith for their prayers to be answered. Perhaps if they could pray as well as they can see, then there wouldn't be the problems which divide.

Find out the names of the pastors and churches within your community. Pray for them. Hear the promise of the Lord for them. Speak prosperity to them. Ask the Lord to revive the pastors as well as the churches. Become a light that drives the darkness from them.

You **can** do this. I won't kid you, it is hard work. There is every opportunity to walk away shaking your head and determine they will never get themselves straightened out. Refuse the urge. Work at that for which you have been fashioned. That is why you live where you do. Be a net mender. Reach out through prayer to your community.

THE PROMISE...OF WORK

Jesus called His fishermen with a promise, **"Follow me, and I will make you fishers of men,"** (Matthew 4:19). They had demonstrated their work discipline in the long days beside the Sea of Galilee. The net destroyers, the ones who would not mend their nets, were not there when Jesus came by. He was looking for men to whom He could teach the work discipline in the light of eternity. Jesus found men who worked for that which perishes. They would learn to work for that which would never perish.

The disciples saw Jesus work miracles and knew these were the "works of God." This prompted their question, **"What shall we do, that we might work the works of God?"** Jesus responded to them, **"This is the work of God, that you believe on him whom he hath sent"** (John 6:28-29).

When we see how far our nation, or any nation for that matter, has wandered from God, the area of ministry to which Christ is calling us seems very large indeed. When John Hyde went to India, the total ignorance of the love of Christ overwhelmed him. He began to pray with a fervor borne of the Holy Spirit. After several years he became ill. On consulting with the doctor, an incredible fact was discovered.

"Hyde, what type of strenuous labor do you perform?" the doctor asked.

"Why do you ask?" responded the man of prayer.

"Your heart has turned over in your chest from the strain of exertion," replied the doctor. "You must move very heavy burdens."

THE NEXT LESSON

This is the **work discipline**. There are millions left to be reached in India, but millions have gone on to eternal life through the prayers of John Hyde. Few have labored as hard in prayer for the Gospel.

With your worship, Word, and work discipline secure, you are ready to go to war. You are ready to disciple a whole nation. You are ready to prayer walk the town; but, where do you go? Our next chapter will become your road map to your testimonies of victory. You are about to learn a little about wrestling the Four Forces from the lives of your friends and neighbors.

CHAPTER 18

Five Pressure Points

"Where do I park the ark?" Good question! My older son Sam wrestled Greco-Roman style for a time. This Olympic sport requires a very strong upper body. The object of this sport is to pin your opponent to the mat and keep him there long enough to win. In like manner we wrestle with the spiritual forces of the Enemy and exercise our power of restraint over the Four Forces they employ in their quest to interfere with the work of the Lord.

Sam and I used to enjoy practicing some of his wrestling moves in the living room of our home. Actually, he practiced, I simply tried to survive. My wife Ellie insisted we remove the furniture to give her larger male types adequate room. Having set the stage, we would wrestle to exhaustion, generally mine, in this ancient sport.

One of the first things Sam was taught was the location of several key pressure points. These are places on the body where nerves and blood vessels are very near the surface of the skin. Pressure applied to these points results in the loss of strength and force in that limb.

If you press the point of the thumb of your left hand into the flesh between the thumb and index finger of your right hand, you will experience the releasing pain of a pressure point. There is also a place on the large trapezius muscle, to the right and left of the neck, (remember the "Spock pinch"?) which is a very familiar pressure point to Sunday School teachers and all those who work with adolescent boys. One little squeeze there and attention is restored.

As we wrestle with the Four Forces of spiritual wickedness, we apply pressure to the five pressure points that will change a nation. Press hard enough and Satan will lose his grip.

CENTERS OF GOVERNMENT

The first pressure point where we park the ark is the **Centers of Government.** Think with me; how do the *archas, exousias, kosmokratos,* and *ponerias* manifest themselves at this center? Can you think of specific instances of intimidation, right to speak issues, abuse of power for gain, or malice emanating from this location in your city? Maybe it is the city hall, or the city council chambers.

Remember, as an Attack Lamb you are not relying on political power to make change. You are going to go to that governmental center and stand in the gap between this pressure point and God for the release for the people. I like to walk around the building. Maintaining my focus on Jesus, I circle the building in prayer.

When I did this in Moscow it took a full hour to walk around the Kremlin. I was not interested in discerning a specific antichrist spirit. Moscow in the Spring of 1985 was the seat of communist atheism and filled with the antichrist spirit.

On location, I began to praise the Lord. Our conversational relationship, developed through so many prayer and praise sessions, resulted in insight. The Lord brought to mind that one word of truth would dispel a lie. I repeated softly, "There is a God. He has a Son. His name is Jesus. He died for me."

Speaking such a thing in the face of the forces arrayed there evidently applied pressure. The truth negated the implied power of intimidation and I felt no fear at all. I walked and rejoiced as the Lord affirmed my proclamation of truth with His peaceful Presence. He sent the blessing of peace.

Encouraged by the closeness of His Presence, I entered the Kremlin and took a position in the rose garden across from the executive office suit. Later I found out I had been only a few meters from Mr. Gorbachev's office. That early Spring morning, my mind was filled with the song, "I come to the garden alone, while the dew is still on the roses; and the voice I hear, falling on my ear, the Son of God discloses. And He walks with me, and He talks with me, and tells me I am his own, and the joy we share as we tarry there, none other has ever known." (*In The Garden*, C. Austin Miles, 1912)

There was power in my praise. No shout needed to be given, no railing against the Devil, just a focused faith on Jesus and the gentle declaration of His Person in that garden. My repose was interrupted by the tower clock.

MOSCOW TIME

In those years the entire Union of Soviet Socialist Republic operated on Moscow time. Even in the vast expanses of Siberia, at least one clock was tuned to the Kremlin tower. It was the pace maker of the heartbeat of Mother Russia. Of incredible significance, it now interrupted my song.

"How convenient," I thought, *"this clock can set the pace for my prayer."* The tower bell would ring on the quarter, half, and hour marks, perfect timing for the Dick

Eastman hour of prayer. I sat and prayed for the first quarter hour that the Lord would send **workers** into the USSR. I prayed for those underground workers whom we had met in ministry and thought of the tremendous shock it would be to Stalin to find out he had not eliminated Christians in a generation, but in fact had only served to cause them to increase. Had he been a student of history, he would have left the Church alone.

The bell sounded the quarter hour and I shifted to the second point of the Eastman hour. "Lord, open the **doors** to this great land that the Word of God may flood in here and wash away the lie of communist atheism. Defeat the horse and the rider."

This was the Spring of 1985. The Lord met me in that garden as I parked the ark. I had a vision of a great open door to the USSR and the downfall of the government so that the Gospel could be preached in every part of the land. I claimed Ephesians 3:20,

> **Now unto him that is able to do exceeding abundantly above all that we ask or think, according to the power that worketh in us, unto Him be glory in the church by Christ Jesus throughout all ages, world without end. Amen.**
>
> **Ephesians 3:20**

I let my thoughts grow bigger than current events, bigger than eschatology, bigger than the Cold War, bigger than the currently available resources and began to be so very happy as the Lord again confirmed His Word with His Presence. What a rose garden experience!

At the half hour I shifted to the third part of the Eastman hour. "Lord, give **fruit** for the ministry." I knew from carrying Bibles to Siberia that there was already a move of God on the university campuses. I had heard about groups throughout Eastern Europe who were hungry for the Word and had a strong prayer life. I thought of the blood of the martyrs calling out from under the altar. The urgency of their cry gave impetus to my prayers. The fifteen minutes flew by so rapidly that I was startled by the tower bell as it pealed the third quarter.

The fourth quarter of the Eastman hour is **finances**. As I called upon the Lord to move in the realm of finance I had no idea that the chemotherapy of Reaganomics would annihilate the communist hold on these masses of people. All I knew was I had seen women with harnesses about their shoulders pulling wooden plows against the rock hard permafrost of the frozen tundra. I had seen men and women huddled together in huge, empty buildings with neither past nor future, mired in poverty's paralysis. I had seen the "black market" whose real street value bore stark witness to the lies of communism.

THE PROCLAMATION

I came away from that rose garden with a proclamation from the Lord. Communism would fall in the USSR and the Church must prepare to rush through the open doors the Lord would give. This was not a welcome message to a Church steeped in Western philosophy regarding the "Cold War." Many rebuked me as unlearned in end-time teachings. I was called aside for correction on several occasions, but continued to proclaim, "Jesus will break through in Russia; you better be ready."

We raised up prayer teams for the capitols of the Soviet republics and soon heard of many ministries mobilizing for intercession. As these Attack Lambs went out, they carried a promise that Jesus would hear their prayers. He is faithful concerning His promise. He answered their cry and in 1991, their persistence was rewarded with open doors, fruit, and more finance than mission history has ever seen.

Intimidation fled. Right to speak was given back to the Church. The materialism of the ruling communist six percent was overthrown. The malice against Christians ceased and the weapons of malice began to be destroyed. How could such a thing happen? Christians had mobilized in prayer teams. They had followed the example of Jesus who walked from city to city proclaiming the kingdom of God.

As you enter into the center of government of your country or travel on a prayer journey to another land, know that history affirms what you are doing. Get in there. Park the ark. Praise the Lord. Hear from Him. Do as He says and you will see your prayers answered. The Lord is faithful.

CENTERS OF COMMUNICATION

The second pressure point is **Centers of Communication.**

I was sitting in the Forum Hotel in Warsaw. The trip from Beijing via the Trans-Siberian railway had left me temporarily without funds and, with the few dollars I had, I had purchased beef tartar. That dish consists of an uncooked pile of beef with a raw egg. Not the highpoint of the trip. I was distracted from my feast by the conversation at the adjoining table.

"So, we send the signal up to the satellite and beam it from satellite to satellite until we bring it down in major cities all over the world. The technique is called 'Footprinting'."

"Which network developed the technology?"

"Actually, it was a Christian ministry who introduced it to us. They plan to use it to hold an evangelistic rally in one city and to reach the whole world with it at the same time."

A Christian ministry setting the pace in communication? I was so excited. Thank God for TBN! The Power Lifting Championships were going to be broadcast through technology invented for the Gospel!

For nine years Pastor Russ and Norma Bixler held fast to a vision for a Christian owned and operated television station for the city of Pittsburgh, PA. They prayed and walked about the land for the station. They called the Church to pray. They remained faithful to the things the Lord showed them to do. Their prayers were answered and Cornerstone Television came to pass. Through the ministry of CTV souls are won around the world. Now, with uplink capability, they are praying for the day that they can "footprint" to the nations.

As you identify the centers of communication to prayer walk in your community, do not stop with just the radio and TV stations.

I personally believe that MTV is the Enemy's number one ballistic missile against this generation. I strongly urge you to find which of your local stations carries it, and find the location of your cable operator. Remember, gentle as lambs, go and pray. Pray as though the destiny of your children was at stake. God will meet you there.

Finally, newspapers are still most effective in small towns and the community grape vine operates very well.

Find the center. Park the ark. Focus on Jesus through praise. Pray for insight. Pray according to the insight He gives and keep it up until you sense the breakthrough. That wonderful release will come as you remain focused on Jesus.

CENTERS OF EDUCATION

The third pressure point is **Centers of Education**.

As the saying goes, "Whoever holds the children holds the future." With this declaration the red-scarfed pioneers of communism were launched. You must park the ark at centers of education. They were intended to carry the message of communist atheism into world dominance in their generation. Do you know who prevented it from happening? Read on.

We were standing in the Orthodox church in Novosibirsk. It was a bitter cold, Sunday morning, but the place was packed. This Siberian city had been created as the center for academic excellence for the emerging generation of Soviet leaders who would take Russia beyond the moon and stars.

To stave off the bitter cold I stuffed my hands deep into my pockets. I lifted my eyes to the ornate facade above the altar. There in silver and multicolored brilliance the Gospel message stood forever in the gilded characters of fourteenth-century Russia. With a sense of the abiding power of the faith, I prayed.

Suddenly my reverie was shattered as my hands were forcefully yanked from my pockets. Looking beyond the knurled finger thrust at the end of my nose, I saw the steely blue eyes of my first Russian babushka up close. This grandmother of the faith wanted me to know that in the presence of God, I had better keep my hands out of my pockets.

I looked deeply into those eyes. What had she seen? Had she been driven here by Stalin as a young girl? What was it that kept her faith so very alive? Opening her shopping bag she broke off a piece of the communion bread and offered it to me. I reached inside my jacket and took a Russian Bible and put it in her bag. I have never seen such a smile.

GRANDMOTHERS AND GRANDCHILDREN

After the service, our group was taken to an adjacent building where we witnessed several proud grandmas presenting sons and grandsons to be baptized. In spite of all the intimidation and the complete absence of a right to speak, these women were passing the fire of Christian zeal to the next generation.

We understood at the time that the Church had fifty thousand believers in cell groups. It was 1986 and faith was alive and well in Siberia. The grandmothers made certain their children and grandchildren kept and multiplied the faith. What Stalin promised would happen in a generation had been reversed because of the faithful praying grandmothers of Russia. Though they were sent to die in the frozen waste, they not only survived, but also multiplied the faith.

By the time Russia opened the door to the Gospel there were over a hundred thousand believers in Novosibirsk. They were already organized and had developed a sound curriculum for leadership training. Yes, the New Siberia was the future of the nation, but it was not the future Stalin had envisioned. From this center of education Christian leadership has come for all of Europe.

Russia was not the only country in those years to be impacted by prayer. In the United States, which bans the public reading of Scripture and the Lord's Prayer as well as Christian symbolism in public schools, a group of young people set themselves to meet at the flag pole of the school at the beginning of each school year and dedicate the year to the Lord.

In those school districts where "See You At the Pole" has taken place, teen suicides have decreased, drug sales and usage have decreased, and in many places Bible clubs are being established. Jesus will give the victory to those who pray. We know that if we ask anything according to His will He hears us and grants the petition we desire of Him (John 5:15). The truth is, He is more eager to answer your prayers than you are to pray them.

Any school can be a target for prayer walking: public schools at all levels, trade schools, colleges, and even Christian schools.

Some friends of mine pray for a Hebrew Academy in their town every time they pass it. They raise their hands toward the buildings and speak salvation and a knowledge of their true Messiah to everyone in the school, students, faculty and staff.

CENTERS OF COMMERCE

The fourth pressure point is **Centers of Commerce**. This is the domain of the *kosmokrato*s. Using people to get things is the method of operation for this crippling force. Centers of commerce can include legitimate businesses as well as those not so honest, such as places where drugs are sold. I leave it to you to determine where this force is operating in your town.

On a global scale, I feel that Cali, Colombia, is a center for the *kosmokratos* because of the millions of people who are destroyed by their number one export, cocaine.

Several years ago I was in Cali to visit a fine ministry. One morning I took a walk. Actually I was looking for a place to park the ark and get in touch with Jesus about this force. I walked quietly, focusing on Jesus in praise. I found myself at a small park in the middle of a very well-to-do residential section. Quite accustomed to Latin America, I thought little of the broken glass sills or of the high walls. The barbed wire too was not unusual for those days.

In front of me was a beautiful little lake with beautiful huge willow trees. It was just the sort of morning prayer place I love so much. I sat on one of the cast iron benches and began to commune with the Lord, offering praise. I was soon ushered into worship and was having a really wonderful time as the warmth of a new day complimented the peaceful presence of the Lord.

I was not alone. My right ear filled suddenly with the sound of an automatic weapon being cocked.

"Why are you here?" The question in Spanish was not offered in gentle tones.

I answered quietly and gently in Spanish, "I am here to pray." The responding laughter highlighted the irony of the moment.

"Do you know where you are?" Of course I didn't know in earthly terms, and I really didn't think mentioning heaven was a good idea right then. I shook my head to indicate that I did not.

"Get up....keep your eyes straight ahead.....keep walking.....do not stop....do not come back here!" The terms of release seemed fine to me, and the ark slowly moved away from the pressure point. Yes, you may meet some resistance from those who occupy for the Enemy.

When I returned to the home of my host I told him what had happened and where I had been. His face went pale as he asked me to not go there again nor even leave the house without escort. I had "stumbled" into the central court of four of the very highest families in the drug cartels.

Within a year the man on whose bench I had sat was in jail. Several of the others have died. Drugs still flow from Cali, but I believe if we intercede (enter into that city to pray) we can see Jesus overcome what man cannot.

Commerce has several types of pressure points because it operates on several levels. They are raw materials, manufacturing, distribution sites and end-users. Let the Holy Spirit direct you to exactly where to apply pressure.

CENTERS OF SPIRITUAL ACTIVITY

We have talked about Centers of Government, Centers of Communication, Centers of Education and Centers of Commerce. What is the fifth center? The most obvious—**Centers of Spiritual Activity**. From the text of 1 Samuel 5:1-5 we know that false gods bow down in the presence of the ark. We know that false gods lose their heads in the presence of the ark. When we park the ark in the temples of the false gods, we cause the Four Forces behind them to bow down.

Twenty-five percent of the world's population is Chinese. These wonderful people can be found on the mainland, but also in every major city on earth. Their language and culture remain a mystery to the remaining seventy-five percent of us. We wonder about the dragons and food tastes and think little about the people. It has been said that even if we win everyone else on earth to Christ and fail to reach the Chinese, the highest grade we can get is seventy-five percent...a "C."

I was consecrated to minister among the Chinese through the laying on of the hands of Wang Ming Dao, the father of the house church movement. I had the honor of meeting with him in 1985 in Shanghai. His prayer has seriously altered the course of my life.

In the years of working among the Chinese, my relationship to their centers of spiritual activity has progressed from curiosity through consternation to compassion. They are a people trapped in the past and trying to stretch toward the future. The reforms of communism were designed to move these people from a life of "superstition" to a life of "pragmatic socialism." The new reforms are designed to move them to a sense of "spiritual community." However, the spirit that community is based upon is the human spirit.

CHINESE NAMES...A CLUE

Chinese names are a puzzle to most Westerners. For example, in our home church in Singapore we have Pastors Song, Ong, and Hong. Their full names are Song Mieng Lien, Ong Tian Chuan, and Hong Chi Her. Chances are you just glossed over those names, but if you did, you missed something very important. The point is that a Chinese name will tell you much about the person.

The first word tells you from which part of China their family comes. The second name is a prophetic telling which the monks felt was auspicious for the person. The third name tells you the clan identity and temple to which they pertain. When you know this, you are ready to park the ark.

I was teaching a Prayer Walking Seminar in a

church in Singapore. Of the 1,500 participants ninety percent were English-speaking Chinese. I suggested that they should identify the spiritual centers—in their case, the temples to which their families related—and should park the ark there while holding some small group outreach for the families of that temple. I suggested they bind the generational curses and the familiar spirits which kept their loved ones from receiving Christ.

Saturday afternoon of the seminar the church's pastoral team took a little walk with me. We went to a principal temple in the heart of Singapore. They realized the Power Presence of the Holy Spirit as we parked the ark in front of the ancestral tablets and prayed for the families represented. They told me later that the joy which filled their hearts there in the midst of so many idols, with our lungs burning from the incense, and the stench of rancid palm oil filling the place, was greater than any they had known before.

Within six months the church added one thousand new members. One thousand! The impact of prayer walking and specifically targeting the centers of spiritual activity, combined with evangelistic outreach, has caused such a migration of former Buddhists to Christ that Buddhist chanters have been sent from Taiwan and China to try to stem the flow. You can see them in Singapore placing their little triangular flags on ground that they feel they must recapture.

The pastor of that church attributes the mobilization of his followers to reach their loved ones to prayer walking. There is power in prayer.

WRESTLING THE ENEMY

Every winning wrestler knows the principle of pressure points. Now you do too. Think with me. Where are the centers of government in your town? Pinpoint them and set out a walking course which will cause you to park the ark on that pressure point. The false gods will bow down in the presence of the ark.

Think further. Where are the centers of communication? Try to take a tour or find a way to spend time there. Many television and radio stations offer tours of their facilities. Pray as you go, and then park the ark and release the Power Presence of God. False gods will bow down in the presence of the ark.

Next, identify the centers of education. Whoever holds the children holds the future. You can be most effective in that place. As you pray, there will be changes. If you need instruction, contact us for the two-part video testimony of opening the public schools in America through prayer.

Next, identify the centers of commerce. Remember, there may be types of commerce which are not listed on the Dow Jones industrial averages. Ask the Lord to show you the place to go and pray. Pray for Christian businessmen that they would have the highest profits with the lowest taxes.

Lastly, find the centers of spiritual activity. Do a church walk in your city and ask God to drive the Four Forces from the church and light the candlesticks again. When you see the temples of the Devil in your town, go there and pray. Park the ark; the false gods will bow down for greater is He that is in you than He that is in the world.

When you have identified these five centers, you have identified the principle infrastructure of your city. Now you must invite a few friends to begin to pray for those who live, work, and study in these centers. Take a prayer walk through them and ask the Lord to direct you with specific prayer strategies to reach those souls. As you park the ark there, you will receive not only fresh vision for the place, but also God's direction for reaching the souls there.

Just as the false god bowed down before the ark, so the Four Forces will be neutralized by the glory that dwells in you. Why can't you just stay at home and pray for the places and see change? Because to intercede is to step into the gap. The Holy Spirit is moving in all the earth looking for those through whom He can be glorified. Go on, call some friends and take a prayer walk around a center in your city. You will be amazed at the clarity with which you will hear from the Lord when you meet Him at His place of work.

You are beginning to define your city according to centers of influence, now let's define your nation according to the keys which God has given for reaching it.

CHAPTER 19
Four Culture Keys

Before the days of the 10/40 Window missions emphasis, countries were referred to as Open Access Nations, Limited Access Nations, Restricted Access Nations or Closed Nations. I was always most interested in that last group.

Perhaps it was my parents repeatedly telling me all things were possible to those who believe. It might have been my coach's frequent admonition that attitude, not aptitude, would determine my altitude. It could have been Ann Kiemel's book, *I Love the Word Impossible* (Wolgemuth and Hyatt). Something caused me to believe there is no such thing as a closed country to a praying people. Over twenty years of doing missions has proved it to me.

There is no closed door which cannot be opened. Prayer establishes a beachhead on the Enemy's territory as nothing else can. As George Verwer puts it, "Try the door. If it doesn't open, kick it open. If you can't kick it open, fast till you fit through the key hole. If that doesn't work let the Holy Spirit take you in prayer under the door to the other side."

Now, however, we are now able to go to any culture, anywhere. I have always enjoyed my friend Nick Burt's method of reaching unreached peoples, "Get on the plane to the end of the flight. Get a cab to the bus station. Take the bus to the end of the line and walk down the first street. You will be in the midst of unreached people."

PRACTICING AT HOME

Let's say we are at the local high school, and we have parked the ark. In the ten minutes before the basketball game begins, we park on the bleachers. You don't like basketball? Never mind, you are there to pray for the people. You don't like the people? Well, all the more reason to keep your focus on Jesus.

Looking to the Lord, we softly praise Him. Imagine that, praise in the public high school. This is Attack Lamb stuff. We pray for what? Perception. We need to perceive the Four Forces and how they operate in this place. Now remember, you are on the inside of a "pressure point" so you will discern some pressure. It's natural to be somewhat nervous.

The Lord shows us the forces of intimidation. He shows us the "pecking order" or social structure of the faculty, students, and parents. He shows us the worldliness or *kosmokratos* of the location and event. He causes us to feel "at risk" if there is malice present. Jesus will show you these things as you focus on Him.

We pray, binding these forces. Actually, at this point my wife often takes a little walk around the place, especially if she discerns malice. You see, our sons regularly participate in these events so I am sharing a regular practice of our family.

In this perception time, God will bring many ideas to your mind on how to reach the people in that room.

GOD GIVES THE FOUR KEYS

Several years ago I attended a basketball game at our local high school. My older son Sam was playing, and I was very happy to find the son of Pastor Jay Passavant, one of our SEAPC board members, playing for the other school. Jay and I arrived at about the same time and sat together on the top row of the bleachers. High points are often most effective for parking the ark.

My wife and I had spent hours in that gym. We had supported our two sons throughout their high school years. The Lord had given us particular and specific insight into the lives of each person we prayed for praying. As the different people came in, I shared with Jay the key to reaching each one with the Gospel. In the course of the conversation I realized that the keys to reaching them fell into four categories;

Language Keys
Culture Keys
Humor Keys
Power Keys.

Let's look at how these keys work to unlock various cultures for the Gospel of Jesus Christ.

LANGUAGE KEYS

In every language there is a reference to the Gospel. These are often called **redemptive analogies**. In our work with the Chinese we have been made aware of several of these.

The Chinese have enjoyed a written language for five thousand years. No matter how the characters are pronounced in the various dialects, the meaning is the same to all Chinese in their written form. Imagine, one fourth of the word with the same written language!

The concept of right relationship is basic to everything in Chinese life. The question of right relationship to heaven, to God, is perhaps the most perplexing to the Chinese. They see themselves as very small and creation as very big. You can see in their paintings very small people surrounded by gigantic mountains with waterfalls. Above and larger than the mountains are the clouds of the heavenlies. They often occupy more than a third of the frame.

Three thousand years before Jesus was born, the Chinese created their symbol for right relationship or "righteousness." The root of the symbol, or first part of the character to be drawn, is the symbol for "ego" or "self." The second part of the symbol is a lamb. In Chinese you must "take the lamb for yourself" to be righteous. Three thousand years before the birth of Jesus the Lord gave the prophetic instruction for all Chinese that "righteousness" can be obtained only by taking the lamb to cover the self.

This is a **language key.** When you are sharing with a Chinese you know they are already thinking of the lamb as long as you use the word "righteousness." Often I say to a Chinese person, "You already believe in the Lamb." Then I explain to them how this is so. Or I ask them, "Do you know who the Lamb is?" When they tell me they do not, I ask, "Would you like to know?" When they say yes, I have the perfect opening to share Jesus, the Lamb of God that takes away the sin of the world, and makes us righteous before God.

BACK TO THE GYM

You're not planning on going to China? Well, at least we got you to the gym. What was the language key there? One of the coaches kept yelling the name of Jesus in his frustration. Have you ever heard it? While the practice is very offensive to me personally, it tells me he does not know the Precious Person behind that name.

After the fifth or sixth time of hearing the name

of Jesus mistreated, the thought occurred to me, *"This is a language key. This is something I can capitalize on for souls."*

The next time he shouted, I asked those sitting around me, "Why Jesus, why not Mohammed or Buddha or Shiva? Why does he shout the name of Jesus?" They were dumbfounded. No one had asked the question although they were also uncomfortable with the abuse of the Lord's name.

Into their silence I inserted the answer for them, "Because Jesus is the only One who has true power. He has to use that name because the others have no power. The demons in the Bible called out the name of Jesus in much the same tone." I quietly asked the Lord to deliver that coach from the oppressive spirit which controlled him.

About a year later I saw the man outside the school. He told me he had seen me preaching on a TV show and liked what I had to say. I asked if he had prayed the prayer with me at the end and he said he had.

In the four years since then we have had many close basketball games. He has yelled at players. But not once in all those years have I heard him abuse the name of Jesus. Chinese or American, the principle works. God will give you the language key, and when you slip it into the door of their hearts, you will set the prisoners free.

THE CULTURE KEY

High in the mountains of Guatemala is a small Indian village called Zaqualpa. Several years ago my wife and I were working with a group of missionaries attempting to reach the Quiche people of the region. We flew up to the village in a single engine plane to spend time at a very small mission station there.

My wife and I are both of German extraction so our oldest son's hair was that white silky blonde which adorns the heads of European children. He was just learning to walk at the time. On the mission field we carried him in a back pack frame rather than letting him crawl about in the dust because of the risk of parasites.

The day was fraught with a string of interruptions and much last-minute packing. Finally, we took off and arrived at the village; it was nearly dusk. The pilot buzzed the dirt strip to chase off grazing cows and playing kids. Then, with a tight "hammerhead" type turn we reversed direction and landed out of a huge red sun. Heads spinning, but laughing with relief and joy, we tumbled from the plane and quickly unloaded our gear so the pilot could get back to the city before dark.

I hoisted Sam into his carrier on my back and walked the thirty meters or so to the 3 by 4 meter wooden shed that would be our home for the next few days. Ellie brought armloads of "stuff" for the mission station there, and we were pleasantly greeted by Audrey who lived there.

Getting settled was fun. We had things for Audrey and shared the news from the city and around the globe. She was a wonderful grandmother who was ministering the love of Jesus in those remote mountain villages.

Our socializing was interrupted by the sound of many people outside the building. It sounded as if the place was surrounded and a guerilla war was going on in the region. We became quite concerned.

I was chosen to answer the knock at the door.

As it swung open we could see hundreds of Quiche people. They were dressed up in their beautifully colored earth tones of woven wool. Their jet black hair was braided with beautiful streaming ribbons.

The men were quite small, but appeared very strong. The leader addressed me in a dialect which I did not understand and then in Spanish.

"We have come for you to tell us," he said in a clear dignified voice.

"To tell you what?" I asked, without the faintest idea what he meant.

"The way to God. Our legend tells us that at the

time of the red sun a man will come from the sky carrying a child with golden hair, and he will tell us the way to God. You have come from the red sun, and there is the child of golden hair, and we have all come to hear of the way to God."

I looked at Sam now toddling his way to the door. God had given him to us for a purpose, and a nation would be released because he was the fulfillment of a **culture key**.

We had great success in that place. Doors opened to the people which had been closed for over one hundred years of missions. Audrey went out to the villages and many children were raised form the dead as she prayed. Jesus was lifted up among the Quiche. They still think God lives in the sun, but they know to get to Him you must serve His Son Jesus. Culture keys are some of the most powerful keys to reaching a people for Jesus.

BACK TO THE GYM...AGAIN

As I watched Sam play in that basketball game so many years later, I asked the Lord for the culture key to this society. America is too young to have identified its culture. Many of the keys are going to have originated in other cultures from which this melting pot of a nation has been derived. African-American, Italian-American, Irish-American, European and other cultures have all brought their culture keys to this country.

For the people in that gym the common culture key was a **priority for their family.** I started talking with one of the men sitting near me. We had known each other since childhood. As kids we each had a reputation for violent strength. While he spoke I realized he had been through enough life experience to have been broken. The gentleness which came from his heart was so genuine. We began talking about Jesus, and he quoted his favorite TV preacher. He didn't attend a church, but there was a culture key that could unlock him to serve the Lord. He loves his family. The culture keys to your circle of friends and acquaintances are probably things you value highly as well.

THE HUMOR KEY

When I teach the Prayer Walking Seminar in person, one of my favorite sections is the typology of the ark. You read it inChapter 7. When I stand in front of the people to teach I do hand motions which describe each part of the ark, but without saying anything. When I come to the part about the "pot of manna," I reach with both hands and bounce my stomach. My ample flesh makes for a humorous illustration. The people laugh and laugh, but they do not forget the point. This is a **humor key.**

Much of humor is at the expense of another. It can be very hurtful especially when you are the brunt of the joke. In the gym crowd, everyone loves humor. We take pleasure in being together. A merry heart does good like a medicine (Proverbs 17:22). The happy person brings joy to the place. But, I realize when I'm parked in a pressure point like the gym, I'm in the midst of broken marriages. There can be great pressure as the two new couples come to watch a child play who is in the middle of the families. The Four Forces work extra hard to defeat them.

The Lord has given me a key in this area to defeat the Four Forces. Instead of being critical, I try to be gently kind to those who are hurting. Sharing humor with them often opens the door and communicates your acceptance of them. As a result of the open door created by my attitude, the opportunity to lead several to Christ has softly come. Pray that the Lord will give you a special love and understanding for these folk.

THE POWER KEY

All you need to plant a church is a good miracle.

We were prayer walking on Bintam Island in the Riou Province of Indonesia. (Just follow the equator around and you will find it). A family from the team was invited to a local home for lunch and of course went. Home-cooked Indonesian food is incredibly wonderful.

While they were there they met a lady whose face was being eaten away by leprosy. With no medical facility available for her, she was kept at home. The female team member asked if she could pray for the lady. She was permitted and did so. Then she also gave her a verse about new skin. Nothing appeared to happen so they encouraged the family, thanked them for lunch and went on their way. She shared the experience with us over dinner.

That evening we were in a church and the Holy Spirit was moving. The female team member was standing next to me on the platform as we were all caught up in worship. Focused on Jesus, I was interrupted by her incessant tugging on my shirt.

"Look, Pastor Mark," she said, "there is the lady."

"What lady?" I asked, having only half-listened to her lunch testimony.

"The leper lady," she said.

As we watched, a breeze blew across the woman, and the light pastel veil covering her face was gently whisked aside. Her face shown as tears of love washed across brand new skin. Her nose had been restored as well as her cheeks and ear lobes. Jesus was making her over as we worshiped. We could not speak. We could barely breathe as the anointing of God was so intense. No one called her forward or dared to interrupt Jesus as He touched her with healing.

The news spread quickly and the church has been packed every night since. Four years later, they are opening a training center to send people throughout all of Indonesia. Moslems in that part of the world are coming to

Christ because they have seen the manifestation of a **power key.**

BACK TO THE GYM...ONE MORE TIME

Across the gym is a big man. His powerful 350 pounds glide through the place on a 6'6" frame. He loves every kid on that floor and watches over them like his own. In a wheel chair next to him is his oldest son. He loves Jesus.

Late last October the weather had been bitter cold. I found out the young man was about to have his twenty-something operation. He had been born with tremendous difficulties and had been confined to the wheel chair. His three younger brothers, by contrast, had each been star athletes on a national scale. He has not missed a single game of theirs.

I went to visit him before his operation at the request of his parents. The doctor had not given them a good prognosis. In fact, the feel of death was very much in the air. He and I spent a half hour together and I gave him my pocket cross which I had carried for years. He received Jesus and declared he had experienced a change in his heart. I went on home and continued to pray for him.

His dad told me the rest of the story. They had prepared him for surgery and told both he and the family things did not look good. As they were taking him to the operating room he became very distressed, calling out to his father. Dad leaned in close to him and asked what he wanted. He wanted the cross. He said he wanted to know Jesus was with him as He knew He had been with me so many times. They went back and found the cross and gave it to him.

Now, several months later, there he sits alive and well, next to his father. His recovery is a **power key** which has allowed me an open door to share Christ with student athletes throughout the school. Jesus touched him. His family testifies he is a new person. His language has changed. His attitude has changed. His life has changed.

YOUR TURN AGAIN

As the game ended we rejoiced in the testimonies of the Lord. Jesus loves everyone of these people. We must go to where they are and park the ark. We do not wrestle with flesh and blood. We wrestle with four forces that want to keep them from being saved. You have the indwelling ability as a child of God to go and neutralize the power of the Enemy in your school. You can get in the gap and begin to pray. You can become involved in the life of the place.

How are you going to access your local school? Develop an action plan. Ask your prayer partners to pray for you as you go. Become involved as a volunteer at some level. If this generation is lost to hell it will be because the adults let them go.

How are you going to access your local government? Develop an action plan. Ask your prayer partners to pray for you as you go. Find a place to park the ark. Pray for the people who work there. Make yourself aware of their world. Let the glory of God flow through you to the community.

How are you going to access your local communication center? Develop an action plan. Write letters to the editor, small papers love them. Take out an ad for a place of prayer. Infiltrate through activity. Find a place to park the ark.

How are you going to access the center of commerce? Develop an action plan. Get churches and individuals to rent a store front for prayer. Open a coffee shop. Start a lunch-time prayer walk around the complex. Get a few associates to join you in fasting one lunch a week, pray for the business and the souls in it. Find a place to park the ark and let the glory of God flow through you in it.

How are you going to access that center of spiritual activity? Develop an action plan. Ask your prayer partners to pray for you as you go, and take someone with you. Enter in for the souls of the people. Find a place to park the ark and let the glory of God flow through you and release the people.

The Lord will show you the way for it is His great pleasure to give you the Kingdom (Luke 12:32). He has, after all, given you the keys. To use these keys, you must "enter in" to the gap-like doorways of the world. You can do this because Jesus is the Way. As you pray to be used of Him, remember your feet. Let them be swift to walk in His way.

CHAPTER 20

Opening the Door to a Nation

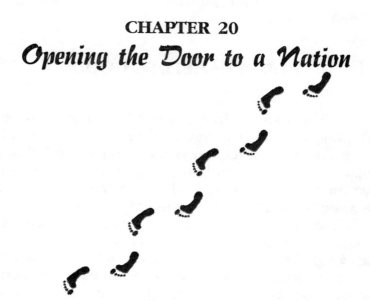

I was sitting on a housetop in Kathmandu, Nepal, talking with our team of eight prayer walkers who had gone trekking to take literature to the western region of the mountain country. After sharing our experiences, it became obvious that, in order to reach our goal, we would have to split up. We had already mapped out the area we were going to, and now we assigned territories. Rick Mains, a man of God from Kansas, and I went with one porter to the snowline while the rest of our group went through a more densely populated area in the direction of India.

Rick and I had climbed to twelve thousand feet and made the mistake of not descending to sleep. As a result, we had difficulty with altitude sickness and circulatory problems. The Lord intervened and we did not fall off the mountain; as a result, the next day we were able to get along at a reasonable pace.

That evening we stayed at the home of a Buddhist trader in the town of Dohrpatan. It is at this town that the mule teams from Tibet and India meet and the cultures transact business. Salt for silk, spices for saddles and so forth. Our host was the middle man for these trades and quite wealthy.

I DIDN'T SMELL SO GOOD

When I awoke in his house I became aware of a very pungent odor. Of course, given where I was at the time it could have been anything. As I sniffed about, I realized it was my own body. I stank. Body odor is not news for anyone who has trekked in Nepal, but this smell was way beyond that. Removing my shoes and socks I was startled to find puss running from several open sores. During the course of our trek I had contracted a local disease called *pani*. This Hindi word for "water" lets us know the bacteria involved are water borne. Actually, they enter through any sore in the feet causing a very serious infection, which spreads rapidly. I tore away dead skin and administered a salve and then wrapped my feet with adhesive tape. With clean socks and new shoes, I felt it would be alright to do our prayer walk that day.

We began to walk that morning and after about an hour had to ford a clear stream. Like true Nepali we just walked into it. The stream was run off water from ice and snow less that a mile away. Its numbing cold gave me some relief to what was already becoming a difficult situation with my feet.

By noon we crested a ridge we would now descend for several days, working our way along granite paths to a roadhead we would take just over a week to reach. Since there are no roads in these mountains, you become accustomed to walks measured in weeks as opposed to hours. In Nepal there is no direct route from anywhere or to anywhere. You just keep climbing either up or down. There is no level ground to be found. After a while, the heart pounding, lung burning "ups" become more pleasant than the knee twisting, toe crunching, gut wrenching "downs." In Nepal everything that goes down must again come up.

THE THIRD DAY

By the third day I knew I was in real trouble. The infection was spreading rapidly. The swelling had gone beyond the limits of the tape, which I determined I would not remove until I couldn't walk any more. My overall health was deteriorating as the infection raced through my blood. Each heart pound sent tiny bacteria to homes where they would build colonies and start pumping waste into my system. Prayer was a groan.

I used a walking stick and, shuffling my feet, I slid along as best I could. My ego was destroyed when I had to give the porter my pack so I could keep up with Rick. My partner had been assaulted with Spina Bifida as a child but was really getting along well, and his great victory left little room for my complaint. We must have been a sight.

After two more days we reached a village along the bank of a good-sized little river. We would stay here and, I was told, it was just one full day's walk to reach a place where we could get a bus back to Kathmandu. Relieved, I lay down on a bed made from a wooden door in the back room of a shack, and dropped into the deep sleep of the exhausted. I awoke a short time later with the strange feeling something was eating me, and when I inspected myself I found hoards of bed bugs feasting on me.

When morning mercifully came upon us I was the picture of misery and disgust: filthy, unshaven and bug infested, inside and out. I was determined, however, and we began our last day's walk. I crossed the river without feeling the coolness of the water at all. In fact, my reddened upper legs told me something disastrous was about to happen to my already sorry state.

TIRE TRACKS

As we emerged from the river, there in the silt at the river's edge was a most wonderful sight. A tire track. Never before or since have I so enjoyed the appearance of a tire track. And this one was not alone! There were more. It was a group of tire tracks. Saved!

"Where there are tires, there are wheels," I explained to the guide. "Where there are wheels there are vehicles." My excitement built as he stared at me. "Where there are vehicles one does not walk, one rides!" My joy was lost on him. He had been paid to guide us on a walking trek, and didn't understand why we wanted to ride now.

"We walk just half day and be there," he insisted.

"No, man, we sit and vehicle come and carry us." Was there pleading in my voice?

"Just six hours, very close." He turned and started on the trek.

I sat down. Sitting down is the "full stop" of many cross-cultural communications. Just sit down. He got the message and came and sat beside me. His concern was he had been hired to travel the distance on foot and to bring us safely through. I was ill, we were going to ride instead of walk. He was afraid of losing face as a guide. I assured him I would put plenty of face back on him by telling the world he was a wonderful guide, and that none of my plight was his fault, and I thought he was a great guy, and now couldn't we please ride?

We worked it out.

OUR TAXI COMES

The vehicle that came was a Chinese tractor pulling a wagon. It was our taxi to the next town. We took it. Three hours later we all arrived.

By now it was late afternoon and Rick and the guide went to buy our bus tickets. I sat down on a bench under a rough lean-to and, knowing I wouldn't have to walk anymore, gave my feet some well-deserved attention. I was joined by three street beggars. My appearance must have put them off for they did not even ask me for alms.

The two men wore filthy cotton shirts and rag skirts. With them was a young woman. She was filthy. Her hair was matted with live-in dirt and bugs. Her filth-encrusted face rested atop shoulders covered only by the ragged remnant of a man's undershirt. On her hip was a naked baby who was equally filthy. This sight will never leave me. They just stared at my feet. They knew what was wrong with my feet, and they also knew I probably wouldn't have them long. I could see the pity in their eyes.

GOD'S OPEN DOOR

When I removed my first shoe, I was nauseated by the stench. They stood back a bit, this odor overcoming their own, while I removed the now shredded sock and took hold of the tape.

Have you ever pulled adhesive tape from skin? Can you imagine the dead skin and tissue coming with it? As I pulled the final layer, puss flew in every direction. My feet burst into the air. I think all the flies of India converged on that rotten flesh.

The young girl reached out to touch my feet. Tears washed rivulets down her dirty, crestfallen cheeks. Her tears fell to the dust before me, and her hand of compassion reached across culture and time to comfort me. I was ministered to by the lowest of the low caste of Asia. God had brought me lower than the lowest that I might have ministry among them.

I would never forget them, nor they me.

God had opened the door.

JOURNEY OF FAITH

I did what I could to bind up my feet again and, tickets in hand, we boarded the bus. As we pulled out of the village I waved good-bye to my three friends. I didn't know it then, but I had just started on what would be the longest journey of faith I have ever taken, even to this day.

They delivered me to the Mendies Haven hospital in Kathmandu. At first the doctors thought they would have to remove both of my legs above the knees. Not a good prognosis for a prayer walker. Much prayer was offered by the whole team. The doctors examined me again and reconsidered. Now they were going to remove them just below the knee. More prayer was offered. My legs and feet began to heal. The infection retreated and began to leave.

I took antibiotics regularly and Indira, a wonderful worker at the Haven, ministered to my feet. She pulled away the dead and decaying tissue and applied topical antibiotics regularly. The Lord intervened to do what the doctors were sure was beyond their power to do, and I was healed.

My journey of faith was complete, and behind me was an open door to India. I would return soon to walk through it again.

CHAPTER 21
The Vision and The Strategy

Back on the roof in Kathmandu, near the close of my time in that city, the Lord had allowed me to see a vision.

I saw the beautiful Kathmandu valley filled with a dark cloud. Above the cloud was brilliant sunshine. Beneath the cloud was total darkness.

"What is this?" I asked the Lord in prayer.

"This is the way the world is," He said clearly. "Above the cloud is the way I want it to be; I want to bless all people everywhere. Below is the way they live, in darkness."

"What is the cloud?" I asked.

"The cloud is what separates them from my blessing," He said. "It is sin and religious systems."

"What shall I do?" I asked.

"Be a mobile earth station," He said.

I'm not sure what I expected His response to be, but that was surely not it.

A mobile earth station is a television transmitter which sends the signal to the satellite. The signal is then beamed down to an area where it can be received by a dish or another earth station. The area in which the beamed signal can be picked up is called the satellite's "footprint." Earth stations are very big, pulled by trucks and very heavy.

"Lord, I cannot carry a TV station around the world," I said.

"Not TV," He replied, "prayer! You go where I show you and pray. As you pray I will respond from heaven. When we effect an uplink I will send government-changing revival."

"Where do I go first?" I asked.

"Go to Beijing and take the train across Siberia to Moscow," was the reply.

I agreed to do it, and began planning for the trip. The Scripture the Lord brought to mind was Psalm 119:105, **"Thy word is a lamp unto my feet...,"** which were now totally healed.

It was the fall of 1985 and for the next three and a half years, my family and I went to Asia ourselves, or sent trained teams of intercessors to Moscow and the Trans-Siberian region. As we all know, the Lord did, in fact, send government-changing revival to the USSR. It didn't happen overnight, but it did happen!

THE DIVINE MANDATE

At the time I received the earth station vision, it was against the law to become a Christian in Nepal. The penalty was one year in prison for converting, three years for leading someone to Christ, and six years per person for water baptism. Yet, in the face of these restrictions, the Lord is faithful concerning His promise. We have a divine mandate to walk the earth. With that mandate we have the promise that He will give us the land.

The Lord moved on the Prime Minister of Nepal, and then the King and now you can become a Christian, plant a church, or even preach in the street. We have freedom.

When we go forth with faith in the One who has called us, all things are possible. There is no such thing any more as a "Closed Country." There is no "Closed City." You can get a visa to visit Mecca, put on the right clothes and walk that place for Jesus. You can believe God and take New York City.

God is going to add to your account in heaven every soul which is won as you walk your neighborhood. Each place you go He will breakthrough for you.

Even your city can be taken for Christ. Yes, even yours. To win a city you must have a strategy. Let's learn a little about how it's done.

THE STRATEGY

There is a very simple strategy which will guide us in taking the promised nations.

First, we have to **map it out**. I thank God for AD 2000 and Global Harvest ministries. These people, and the Joshua Project, have teams over all the earth cataloging people groups and finding the four keys to release them. Just a few years ago we had prayer walking teams throughout the 10/40 Window. The year before YWAM celebrated the completion of a phase of their commission with the Cardinal Points Prayer Day.

Next, we must **determine the gateway cities and centers** in the earth. This is being done, but more workers are needed. Get a couple of partners, trust God for the tickets, get a visa and get out there. Walk that land; God is going to give it to you.

After we discern the gateways, we have to **do research.** I was recently in Ankor Wat in Cambodia and discovered there are lines of control which extend from that city to Bali, Indonesia, and then to Dashankali, Nepal. Many are researching the influence of the Four Forces which have prevented the Gospel from reaching the people within this triangle. Recently, we brought teams to the prayer summits of China and coordinated prayer throughout that vast land. We had to leave one peak of the five untouched because we did not have the manpower to get there. We must see God's plan and get in it.

Then, we need to **apply the knowledge** the Lord is giving. I thank God for the networks that are being established. The Body of Christ is coming together through the Internet and we are able to rally multinational teams to meet at specific prayer points and create those uplinks all over the world. You must become involved in the flow of what the Lord is doing. Ignorance is not bliss when the voice of the trumpet calls you to come up to a new level and see the purpose of God.

The Body of Christ has, finally, come to the point where we can **evaluate one another's work with a heart to help.** Self-protective territorialism and self-exaltation are passing from the scene as we see the One who sits on the throne, and get free from self. Finally, the Body is working in unity, bringing racial reconciliation around the world.

Each of us must walk in the synergism of spiritual unity. You have a part to play. You are important in all that God is doing. You are the fulfillment of His power picture.

You are an Attack Lamb for Jesus.

Move with the flock!

WHAT GOD IS DOING

For a moment let's follow Joshua into the promised land. In spite of God's promise to give Joshua every place where his foot shall tread (Joshua 1:3), living that promise was a difficult task. Remember, Israel had been a nation of slaves not conquerors.

To make matters worse, one of the Israelites kept some of the spoil for himself from the first city they attacked. One man's greed broke the ranks of the entire nation, bringing not only defeat in the next battle but disgrace for his tribe and his family. Instead of everyone receiving the fullness of the promise, one man stole a few treasures for himself, only to lose them, and his life and family later.

Today the Lord has brought together many of the mainstreams of Christianity into a unified network of prayer. This has not been accomplished through the work of one or more key men. Instead, God has spoken very gently and providentially to individuals world-wide and caused them to walk to the same goal. The sense of unity is pure not contrived. The openness to work together comes from a common focus on the throne of God.

Within the fibers of this network we find similar patterns. They are the genetic strands of global harvest. Guess what? You are a part of that. Your interest in this book, and the topics it touches, indicates a God-given desire to be part of His plan for these days. I welcome you to the fellowship of mobile intercessors who are taking the land for the resurrected Jesus.

FIVE PRACTICAL POINTS AS YOU GO

We must move in order and at the pace of the whole net. Here are five practical points I have learned in over twenty years which help keep me in the timing and flow of the whole. I share them with you, not to give you a strict method or put you under any bondage, but as principles which help keep me focused on the throne and safe from counterattack.

1. The Lord sent them out in pairs. Let's be smart and do the same. The Christian marriage is God's number one weapon in spiritual warfare. My wife and I have celebrated twenty-six wonderful years of marriage. We are in agreement on God's plan for our lives. We are focused on the throne and desire His will beyond all else. Our home is dedicated to serving Jesus.

Because of my mission's travels we are apart much of the time. Yet, as parents of teenage children, we feel one parent should be at home. Yes, I trust my sons. Yes, I trust the Lord. But, I also trust the Enemy to be the Enemy. As a result, many of my prayer journeys are made with people other than my wife.

The Lord has knit me to several men who also have a heart to see the nations reached. When it is not possible for my wife to travel, one or more of these men join me in targeting a nation. Once a year I lead a large group which includes men and women. I try to arrange it so that my wife and sons are with that team. The principle of family unity is vital to our success.

As a mobile ministry team, we realize each of us has a part to play. I have learned the Lord can, and generally will, speak through any team member at any time. Remember, it was a young musician who had the word for Jehoshaphat and the children of Israel (2 Chronicles 20).

So, let's glean a little from this. Your spouse is God's first choice for a prayer partner. If you don't have a spouse then a same-gender partner should be your choice. Before you go on specific prayer walks into the pressure points to wrestle the Four Forces, you should have gone through the process of developing a prayer partnership with someone you trust completely, both personally and spiritually.

Of course you can pray by yourself. Of course you have a daily prayer life, and your own time of intimacy with Jesus. I am talking about when you target a perceived pressure point, and you are going into it for the purpose of releasing the people under its influence, then you need a partner.

2. You must be specific in your mapping. The initial prayer walk should be one of exploration and identification, a leisurely walk through town with your spiritual antenna up. On our central Singapore route, I walked it first and then invited intercessors from different churches to walk on different days. I did not share the findings of one group or my personal impressions with another group. The groups were diverse; Methodists, Anglicans,

Pentecostals, charismatics, and Lutherans. They each perceived exactly the same pressure points and gateways. It was amazing!

From that mapping we were able to send two-person teams to the pressure points while the others prayed for them. In Singapore you cannot have a group of more than five without a permit. We found teams of two and four worked well for us. But they were disciplined enough to go to the specific points mapped and confirmed by those who had gone before.

In this way the Lord allowed several streams to "own" the prayer vision. Working together, they cast the net in the heart of the city. The Christian population of Singapore has increased so much in five years the Parliament had to publish a "White Paper" concerning the revival's impact on the balance of ideologies on the island!

Asia Week published an article on the revival's impact on business in the region. Centers of government and commerce have been impacted by two people standing on a corner in a completely irrelevant fashion with an uplink to the throne of God!

3. Discipline yourself to a specific report format. There are many available through Global Harvest Ministries, P.O. Box 63060, Colorado Springs, CO, 80962-3060. It is most important that we avoid time-wasters and nit-pickers in a report form. Essentially, what needs to be in a report is where you went, what you perceived, how you prayed, advice for those who will follow and any specific prayer direction you took. When you compile the findings of all the teams you see the multitude of counsel with which there is safety, and the assurance of victory.

4. Volunteer the information of your plans to your pastor to maximize your effectiveness in prayer walking. He will appreciate the information. As a pastor, I always appreciated knowing where the active ministries of our church would be. It gave me the opportunity to pray for them, to watch for books and tapes that would encourage them in their ministry, to drive by that location and encourage them in the course of my duties, and to be ready to answer the phone should the police call wondering why several of our members were walking around their building.

As a result of this pastoral involvement, I have seen the Lord do wonderful things in foreign nations and in the US. We have stressed that we are one Body, and if you, as a member of that Body, are involved in expanding the Kingdom, then we are all involved. Please take the time and make the effort to inform your pastor of the places in which you are praying. You never know, he might just show up one time to encourage you.

5. Develop prayer partner support. There are those who are not going to go out on the streets of your city to pray. You have to be willing to accept that and love them anyway. They might be confined to their homes by illness or responsibility. They might work incredible hours to make ends meet. You must not make them feel like lesser citizens in the Kingdom because they cannot get out and walk with you.

I spend much of my time walking among totally Christless people in nations which try to prevent the preaching of the Gospel. If there is anyone on earth who has cried to the Lord for workers in the face of such harvest it is me. But I tell you, you cannot become estranged from the Body of Christ as an intercessor or you will end up with a small group of pseudospiritual people casting the demons out of each other, and totally distracted from the throne of God. If you love Him, you must love His Church.

Therefore, find a way to recruit members of your church or cell group to become a part of your prayer team. Inform them of the goals of your team, such as, "We are praying together for the principal of our local school to receive Jesus. Please, while you are microwaving your popcorn at the office, take the four minutes of wait time and join us in this prayer time." Or, "As you drive to work you will pass through the very congested intersection at the bridge. Your delay will be about five minutes. Please use these five minutes to pray for a visitation of the Spirit of God on our community." Or, "As you take your child to daycare, please pause to pray for their safety and for the evangelization of all the children in daycare centers in our community. Please pray for centers of education; whoever holds the children holds the future."

Use a few examples that embrace rather than divide. Not everyone has the freedom and ability you have to serve the Lord, so please allow Jesus to give you more great ways to embrace them into prayer ministry.

THE GREATEST NEED

Often I am asked, "Mark, what is missing in the Church today?" More than anointing, more than finances, more than vision, more than leadership, I feel our greatest need is **perseverance**. Hebrews 6:12 gives us the key to receiving the promise of the nations. **"Be not slothful, but followers of them who through faith and patience inherit the promises [of God]."**

As we walked and prayed for Nepal, the forces of resistance were great. The power of government and malice were set against us. In 1983 the Lord declared that He would break through. In 1985 He showed the power of the "uplink," and in 1990 He changed the government. Today you can preach Christ openly in Nepal.

In 1985 God promised change in Russia. In 1988 He confirmed the "uplink," in 1991 the government changed and today you can preach Christ openly in Moscow.

Through those years many thousands—that's right, thousands—of intercessors have been led to travel in those lands and pray. Many have been burdened, have made the choices and gone. Perhaps you have been, or have supported, one or more of them. In these cases the results did not come quickly. If we think of the grandma in Novosibirsk, it has been a prayer time since the fifties.

But God is faithful concerning His promises. He does watch over His Word to perform it. What He says will come to pass.

Pastor Wang Ming Dao spent over twenty years in prison believing that one day he would see China free from the atheistic rider of the communist horse. He died never having seen the fulfillment. He imparted a calling to many and they continue on. China is now 10% Christian and some reports say that 35,000 people a day are coming to Christ. Pastor Wang is part of that great cloud of witnesses who watch us walk and pray. His tears and prayers for China are before the throne, mingled with yours and mine. We shall see the day he envisioned!

Persevere for your city. Persevere for your loved ones. Steve Lightle, a wonderful intercessor for the Soviet Jews, once said to me, "Mark, you will succeed in prayer ministry only if you don't have to have something happen every day to keep your faith up. If you can just see Jesus and His promises, you will persevere until you receive your answer."

Faith is the key to all the strategies of God. Prayer walking, interceding in the gap and being an Attack Lamb is no exception.

ENDNOTES

Chapter 8 - "KNOW YOUR ENEMY"

1. Discussion of the *archas, exousias, kosmokratos* and *pneuma tae ponerias* is based on insights gained from the *Theological Dictionary of the New Testament* by Gerhard Kittel and Frederich Gerhard, William B. Eerdmans Publisher, © October 1994.

2. Strong, James. *Strong's Exhaustive Concordance of the Bible.* "Hebrew and Chaldee Dictionary," "Greek Dictionary of the New Testament." Nashville: Abingdon, 1890. "Greek," entry #746, p.16.

3. Strong, "Greek," entry #1849, p.30.

4. Strong, "Greek," entry #2888, p.43; and entry #2902, p.43.

5. Strong, "Greek," entry #4189, p.59.

Chapter 12 - "AND AGAIN I SAY REJOICE"

1. John Lennon, *Imagine,* Apple Records, Copyright 1971, Maclen Music, Inc., BMI, SW-3421

Chapter 14 - "A FRESH WORD"

1. W.E. Vine, *Vine's Expository Dictionary of Old and New Testament Words,* Thomas Nelson Publishers, © 1984, 1996

Chapter 15 - "DAWN OF A NEW DAY"

1. *What A Friend We Have In Jesus,* lyrics by Joseph M. Scriven, music by Charles C. Converse, public domain.

About the Author

Mark Geppert was selling insurance to a Baptist pastor in 1970 when the Holy Spirit touched his life in an irrevocable way. Under careful training, he began walking out the call of God in his life. Leaving business in 1973 he received Bible and ministry training in the Assemblies of God at Western Pennsylvania Bible Institute.

From there Mark and his wife Ellie went to Guatemala where for three years he directed the Guatemala Assistance Project. Their first son, Samuel, was born in Guatemala.

In 1979 God spoke to Mark to return to Pittsburgh, Pennsylvania, and serve the Church in the establishment of the Dayspring Bible Training Center which opened its doors in 1980. A second son, Matthew, was born in Pittsburgh.

Mark served as Co-Pastor, Missions Director, and Bible Training Center Director until 1988 when he accepted a call to serve as Vice-President and Director of Operation Unreached with the Association of International Missions Services in Virginia Beach, Virginia.

In 1991 Mark and Ellie established the South East Asia Prayer Center. Committed to "Creating New and Networking Existing Prayer Cells in South East Asia," this foundation has brought forth fruit in many nations. Much of their success has been accomplished through Mark's Prayer Walking Seminar which has been taught to more than 50,000 in Asia, both through live conferences as well as audio and video cassette.

Now 50, Mark has lived the principles of prayer. His life is a testimony to the faithfulness of Jesus to those who walk with Him. The focus on Asia continues with works in many nations.

To contact Mark Geppert,
write:

South East Asia Prayer Center
Post Office Box 127
Oakmont, Pennsylvania   15139

Please include your prayer requests
and comments when you write.